Sacred Life, Holy Death

THE ALCHEMY OF LOVE
A Pilgrimage of Sacred Discovery
by Robert Boldman
Heartsfire Books, 1998

Anthologies which have featured Robert Boldman's
poetry and haiku:

BENEATH A SINGLE MOON
Buddhism in Contemporary American Poetry
Shambala Press, 1991

ENTER THE HEART OF THE FIRE
A Collection of Mystical Poems
California State University, 1981

HAIKU MOMENT
An Anthology of Contemporary North American Haiku
Charles E. Tuttle and Company, 1993

THE HAIKU ANTHOLOGY
Haiku and Senryu in English
Simon and Schuster, Inc., 1986

Sacred Life Holy Death

Seven Stages of Crossing the Divide

Robert Boldman

Preface by Khenpo Konchog Gyaltshen Rinpoche

Heartsfire Books

Library of Congress Cataloging-in-Publication Data

Boldman, Robert. 1950–
  Sacred life, holy death: lessons from the near-death experience / by
Robert Boldman.—1st ed.
    p.   cm.
  ISBN 1-889797-22-7 (softcover): $14.95
    1. Near-death experiences.   2. Spiritual life.   I. Title.
BF1045.N4B65 1999   98-42785
133.9'01'3—dc21   CIP

Cover photograph by Loree Boldman, taken at Fountains Abbey, North Yorkshire,
    England, on Easter Sunday, 1996
Cover design by Cisneros Design
Book design and text composition by John Cole GRAPHIC DESIGNER
Printed in Canada
Text is set in Adobe Minion

First edition 1999
10 9 8 7 6 5 4 3 2 1

Heartsfire Books: 800.988.5170
500 N. Guadalupe Street, Suite G465
Santa Fe, New Mexico 87501 USA

E-mail: heartsfirebooks@heartsfirebooks.com
Visit us at http://www.heartsfirebooks.com

If you are unable to order this book from your local
bookseller, you may order directly from the publisher.
Quantity discounts for organizations are available.

More praise for Robert Boldman's
Sacred Life, Holy Death

"Robert Boldman has returned from his journey into death's deep mystery with encouraging insights for us all."

> Merrill Collett, author of *STAY CLOSE AND DO NOTH-ING: A Spiritual and Practical Guide to Caring for the Dying at Home*

"Mr. Boldman has skillfully created a readable, well-researched text that will benefit both clinical professional and lay readers who are interested in learning more about the near-death experience and its impact upon the individual. He offers hope and assurance via authentic case studies and research sources. He utilizes story telling techniques that address basic human doubts and fears and in this way reveals the possibility of a pathway to becoming based upon love.

In my many years of hospice work, I have wished for such a work to share with frightened patients and their families, particularly when they could no longer remain in denial of a terminal diagnosis. There is no doubt that this book will stimulate thought and for many bring comfort as it sharpens their awareness on the journey to knowing. By looking at death, the author brings us full circle to the study of life."

> Diane E. Longeway, LMSW, Hospice Team Leader, University of New Mexico Health Sciences Center

"From the long, slow laboratory of the true heart, *SACRED LIFE, HOLY DEATH* offers clarity and insight for healing unto death that extends our life all the way to God."

> Stephen and Ondrea Levine, authors of *WHO DIES? An Investigation into Conscious Living and Conscious Dying*, and *A Year To Live*

For my mother—

As a prayer for her happiness

CONTENTS

Kabir, a vast ocean is this body,
difficult to fathom its depth;
One who dies while living
and plunges within
earns the rarest of jewels.

—Kabir

by Khenpo Konchog Gyaltshen Rinpoche

I am very pleased to be writing this preface to Robert Boldman's work, *SACRED LIFE, HOLY DEATH: Lessons from the Near-Death Experience.* This book has come together by virtue of the many encounters Robert has had with dying individuals, in both clinical and informal environments. He has cared for these people and looked after them in times of great need. Through these experiences, he has gathered a great deal of wisdom concerning the process of preparation for death's eventuality.

In Buddhism, there is a saying: "The end of birth is death; the end of meeting is separation; the end of collecting is dispersion; and the end of construction is disintegration." The essence of death is distilled here, not as something unusual, but rather as a part of our life's journey. Everyone who is born will have to go through this transformation sooner or later. Seeing that this is so, we recognize the importance of preparation in peace, allowing the most positive of circumstances to manifest during this crucial time. The experience of death cannot be divided among loved ones and friends to share; this threshold has to be passed alone. In order to assist oneself and others in this transition, the practices of compassion and loving kindness are two very special keys to be used, precipitating the transformation of suffering as well as releasing attachment at the time of death.

Without a doubt, this book will help many readers in dealing with the element of death in their lives. It will provide a catalyst for the organization of life's priorities and prepare one for the act of dying whereby others similarly may be benefitted. There are vast numbers of profound books written in the Buddhist world about death and what occurs afterwards. This book contains both the perspective of Western insight and mature investigation coupled with the accrued wisdom of Eastern thought. I embrace this endeavor and hope the book will be treasured by all.

Immediately after formally joining the Buddha's wandering forest monastery, a monk respectfully posed three riddles to the Buddha regarding the nature of the universe. In that age of India's history, such debates were rampant. Hermits thronged pathless regions of India in search of illumination, passionately debating such issues beneath the relentless fires of a tropical sun. They fasted and meditated, passing such riddles back and forth like hot coals. The monk no doubt expected that Buddha was about to untangle these three intricately connected riddles: whether we each have an immortal soul, whether there is life after death, and whether the universe is eternal or finite. However, the Buddha, in reply, posed his own riddle: "Imagine a hunter is wounded by an arrow intended for a deer and is taken to a surgeon. But before he will treat the wounds, the surgeon asks him to describe the man who wounded him: 'Is he tall or short, dark or light-skinned? Is he of lesser or greater caste? Who were his parents and grandparents?' What will happen to this man before these questions are answered?"

The monk could only reply, "He will die, Master."

"So it is with you," the Buddha continued. "Be concerned only with what is relevant to your salvation and with the way it can most expediently be attained. Do not indulge mere doctrines on the nature of God or reality for their own sake."

What Buddha was relaying to his follower was that our doubts about life can never be satisfactorily addressed. Buddha was against idly pondering such matters, not even considering it crucial to determine whether or not there was life after death. Buddha's path was developed as a remedy for this present life's afflictions. He believed that if we cure our existing spiritual maladies, death will take care of itself. He realized that even as the firmament of our beliefs constantly erodes away, the mystery of our spiritual nature is perennial. To accept our spiritual nature as an insoluble mystery, he would surely have asserted, is to finally give birth to wisdom. After all, those three riddles once directed to Buddha are still hopelessly tangled. Such issues remain disturbing to us, even becoming whips that drive us either toward or away from religion. I would like to suggest, echoing the words of this sage infinitely wiser than I, that we surrender to the mystery.

For many years, I have studied death using the near-death experience as my touchstone. In the following pages, I will examine the near-death experience more as a revelation on the way to live rather than solely as a vision of death. If you listen to the thousands upon thousands of testimonies, what you hear is a message of reunion, beckoning us on, encouraging us to love. And I believe what is most relevant about this experience is often ignored—the fact that it addresses our spiritual maladies and illuminates a pattern of spiritual growth. This pattern does not have to be created, it is inherent. Spirituality grows from the firmament of our own consciousness. The near-death experience teaches that if we practice self-sacrifice, the spiritual essence within us will naturally rise. So spiritual growth depends on surrendering to our own mystery—and once the mystery of our own life has been addressed, death takes care of itself.

As a result of illness or mishap, many people have experienced the brief interlude between life and death, a remarkable state during which the entire spectrum of existence is exposed and one's most profound inner depth is revealed. Researchers have compiled many reports which agree on the essential points of what transpires during this experience. Many reports involve a verifiable arrest of normal life signs, usually as a result of cardiac arrest. In some cases there has even been evidence of cessation of all cerebral brain activity. Yet it must be emphasized that these reports may not bear witness to what actually occurs in the *post-mortal* state, but only allude to it. What is glimpsed in the near-death experience, I believe, is a fulcrum point, the instant when life is leveraged exactly against death. The testimony describes a midpoint between life and death, and is therefore uniquely situated to illuminate both, imparting a spiritual wisdom usually hidden from view.

Life has it's cadence, its many rhythms. Consciousness itself is governed by inherent patterns. We are carried daily from our waking state into sleep and dream and back again in a predictable pattern. In a way, we undergo a series of small deaths as layers of consciousness are peeled away. Many psychological theories share the view that dreams are the healer of self, their purpose to make the mind more coherent and whole by representing to us aspects of ourselves which we have forgotten. It has been shown that the more conscious we remain in the dream state, the more vital the images; and here is where we see the visions and hear the stories that are translated into divine myths, here is where our dreams are most spiritually resonant.

Would it not be reasonable, then, to assume that the near-death experience, a much more cataclysmic stripping away of consciousness, would possess these traits amplified? Could not this experience do even more to integrate the competing self-images we each have within us? I believe the cycles of sleep and dream in life are but the reflection of death, the falling in and out of various levels of consciousness in an effort to create a unified vision of ourselves, to unite the layers of mind with their divine core. I further believe this pattern to be intrinsic to the consciousness of all human beings, and that consciousness does not exist apart from these patterns. This motion between deep sleep, dream, and the waking state would then be the most essential rhythm of life, the rhythm to which every other life system and pattern, and finally death, must acquiesce. Sleep could then be viewed as a nightly rehearsal for death.

In the last century science abandoned the notion of a soul. It was not readily apparent nor did it fit into the theories scientists had set in motion, theories which they trusted were the final word. They had discovered that by analyzing life in smaller and smaller pieces, by reductionism, they could uncover many of life's secrets. But they only told us how things were made or how they function, never their meaning or secret. Never why. So the universe was made smaller, ignoring any overall vision. According to such terms, if we are to understand ourselves we must first narrow consciousness so that it fits into the mind, then we narrow the mind until it fits into the brain. We further reduce the brain so it fits into biology, then we reduce that until it fits into chemistry, and finally, this chemistry is reduced to physics, which in turn is looked upon as the foundation of all life. Because the physics of Newton is repetitious and rigidly calculable, the universe came to be viewed as no more than a machine. We became cogs within the machine, the patterns of life wheels within wheels, upon which we are helplessly turning, with no ability to affect our own fate. Such a way of perceiving life is implicitly harsh in its repercussions, as the universe seems loveless and lightless at its heart.

This same mechanized view of life has led scientists to assert that the near-death experience is a random, brain-induced hallucination, as devoid of meaning as the rest of existence. But the near-death experience invariably leads to profound personal growth; it leaves spiritual watermarks on the psyche which redefine and expand our vision of life. The near-death experience, at the very least, seems supremely capable of healing our damaged psyches and putting our lives in order. If the near-death experience is a random event, arising as the result of physical chaos, then it is quite remarkable that a distinct pattern of reintegration and spiritual growth unfolds, rather than meaningless energies and fragmentary images. And while the material secrets science reveals are invaluable, many people are discovering that they cannot lead a satisfactory life without spiritual bearings. I am interested in extracting this spiritual kernel of the near-death experience.

When I was a small child, I accidentally fell into a river and nearly drowned; a brief plunge into the water during which I died and returned to life. It was to become the most significant event in my life, as though a gate within me was left ajar, never to be shut again. Death would involuntarily return to me in years to come, an indelible part of my nature. My life's work has been wholly devoted to probing the mystery of life and death.

Over a span of thirty years, I have worked in hospitals, almost exclusively at the children's hospital near my home. During my early years, with no technical skills yet to my credit, I was often given the task of sitting with dying children, acting as a surrogate father to those who had no family. In those days I also worked in the morgue, assisting with autopsies. Gradually, through the years, I grew acquainted with death's many poses. I spent many years as an emergency-room technician and later, as a registered respiratory therapist, became a member of pediatric and neonatal ambulance transport teams, caring for the critically ill under the most extreme circumstances. I have cared for newborns in birthing wards and a critical care nursery, and have worked many years in pediatric and adult intensive care units, often helping to educate resident physicians in this setting. In this role, I became familiar with the progression of disease and the physical and mental impairment that often follow. I have seen the agonies of despair, sitting beside the beds of the terminally ill, night after night. As I have long worked the night shift, I have found that nighttime, when most family members have gone and fewer care-givers are available, is when the underworlds of fear rise to the surface and the dying person is often most in torment. And I was rubbed raw by these encounters, finding I had to bare my soul in ways I would never have done otherwise.

There were many years when my desperate search into the mysteries of life and death were all that mattered to me. I traveled the country and met with spiritual teachers and followers, and amassed a spiritual library with a world-view of death. I have practiced in many spiritual traditions in my quest for answers. I even went through a period when I remained in bed throughout days and nights when not working, throwing myself completely into meditation on the patterns of consciousness. I could find no answers. Even when literature on the near-death experience did finally begin to reach print in the late seventies, much of my seeking remained fruitless. It was not until a more understandable version of the *Tibetan Book of the Dead* was finally published and I had spent many years working with the dying that an overall vision of the juncture between life and death began to develop. Finally, I was able to see the ways in which the near-death experience and ancient treatises on death, namely those from the East, were in seamless harmony.

More years of study and witnessing many more deaths firsthand led me to begin, tentatively at first, to work with the dying on a spiritual level. I engaged in learning the art of dying with them, as equals. I learned to accept uncritically what each person believed about God. I discovered that it was not one's religion, but the surrender to it, that proved beneficial. I found people died more serenely, seeming heartened, if they were seeking to impart love and gather spiritual wisdom as death unfolded. I found this reflected in my work as well. I engaged many spiritual practices to assist them but found that if I was selfishly motivated, striving to gain some form of merit by assisting them, I grew depressed in my work. I learned to empathize with another's death by taking it into myself, by accepting that what was happening to them was also happening, though more slowly, to me. To let down the barriers between myself and the dying, it was necessary to make myself as vulnerable as they, to let death in. I had to let go of the self I was presently grasping and cherishing. I had to surrender.

It became clear to me that we have no choice but to be transformed by death. And what the near-death experience teaches us is that, in the transition from life to death, all spiritual wisdom is briefly exposed, inviting us to reunite our inner self with the divine, a divine hidden from us only by our contracted self-conceits. Our *self*, ever-changing throughout our lives, is radically changed by death. But we do have a choice in either accepting or resisting this transformation. We can surrender to this process of reunion at death, or we can resist it, seeking to hold on to our familiar self. Death offers us inexhaustible possibilities, but no one fate is assured. If we permit our fears to overwhelm us, a negative death experience usually results; fear and distrust are our greatest enemies at death, fearlessness and surrender, or trust, our greatest allies. To succeed at death and therefore to have ultimately succeeded at life, we have only to surrender to this spiritual process. Mystics, East and West, have echoed what near-death experiencers almost invariably learn: we should not wait until death, we should begin unfolding while still fully awake and alive.

I have written this book in order to translate the near-death experience into a spiritual overview. I will use not only my own near-death experiences but the many reports that are available as well. I will also touch upon such ancient manuscripts as the *Tibetan Book of the Dead* because many near-death experiences, including my own, parallel the teachings in this text. I will also draw upon my work in the hospital, especially with the terminally ill. I am convinced that all we require to attain spiritual fulfillment is encoded within the near-death experience. And this experience sheds the light necessary to see what is awaiting us when life closes and death opens before us. I view this as a beginning point for a dialogue on the near-death experience, not to verify the existence of an imperishable soul but as evidence of our inexhaustible spiritual nature. Only then, I believe, does the near-death experience take root. If Jesus or Buddha were among us, I trust they would argue neither for nor against the validity of these experiences but would seek to transmute them into spiritual sustenance.

I have seen this remarkable transformation in several people who have related to me their near-death experiences. One young person harshly rejected any concept of God or spirituality different from her own, prior to her near-death experience. But afterward, she behaved as though every faith was basking in God's presence. She would ask for books on religion, any religion. She reverently accepted all religions, finding the sutras of Buddha just as uplifting as the psalms of David, but she still prayed most fervently to Jesus, whom she viewed as her savior. He had universality for her, so that she saw his image refracted in the earth's many religions, as though through a spiritual prism. As often happens with near-death claimants, the vision of her faith had grown, yet she did not reject the religion of her birth. Her core beliefs remained the same while the perceived horizons of her religion broadened. Around the core of her most trusted and heartfelt beliefs grew a soft, celebratory sharing, the hard shell of intolerance vanishing.

The near-death experience offers us a glimpse of an afterlife that provides space enough for all religions; like a magnifying lens, the experience enhances our spiritual vision. A vision of unity is grafted to our faith. Death is, we are told, an initiation into reunion with our divine nature.

My work has been to look exclusively at this transformative spiritual process, not to prove or disprove what happens to us *after* death but to examine this brief continuum as a sacred text on spiritual reunion. I have divided this near-death continuum into seven distinct stages, each of which gives a penetrating glimpse of a spiritual awakening. Each of the seven stages, identified for their spiritual significance, can easily culminate in a spiritual realization that is often described as an awakening from the slumber of material concerns. Each stage speaks to us, in very different language, of the awakening from a mortal sleep in which we have spiritually forgotten ourselves. And within each state, we meet with and explore such living symbols of spiritual awakening as lights, heavenly realms, saints, and saviors.

These seven stages possess immeasurable depths into which we delve only to the extent that we open to them from within, parting the waters of our own psyche by an act of surrender, which permits us to both enter that reality and be entered by it.

Like all spiritual paths, each stage has lessons associated with it, so each stage offers us either a realization to seize or spiritual teaching to carry with us. They each describe a different path to spiritual reunion, earlier stages reflecting a meditative path, later ones reflecting more strongly the paths of self-giving and spiritual love. I view no singular path as superior to the others, each being able to spirituality uplift us even to the extent that we reunite with God.

As the book unfolds, I invoke the name of God fairly often, a hopeless but necessary gesture. I am not making reference to any conceivable deity but to the unity that is at the heart of all life. I address this unity, God, as an unimaginable vastness humbling any efforts to describe Him. He is, of course, neither male nor female, nor a spiritual vacuum, but is the Self of all existence, both personal and impersonal, imminent and eternal, empty and full. All that we perceive, I imagine, is His echo. So with the term, God, I gesture rather abstractly toward an infinity disguised as many perishable realities. It is this God, this unity, I believe, that we glimpse during the near-death episode.

I want to emphasize here that you do not need to have the near-death experience yourself to benefit from its revelations. What is important is the overall image that has emerged from this experience. Each person's experience is equally valid, equally crucial in fact, for each encounter contributes vastly to this overall portrait. Only by looking at the portrait that emerges when these reports are collected is our spiritual myopia given a lens through which we can envision the grey, intermediate zone between life and death. Only then do we recognize this intermediate state as a trove of spiritual potentials belonging equally to all of us. We do not need to have experienced a "death" like this for ourselves, nor are the spiritual transformations most of us desire inaccessible—they are a natural unfolding, requiring only trust and surrender to our self nature.

As the *Tibetan Book of the Dead* informs us, there are many passages to God, each of which depends on surrendering a lesser, material self to an immaterial spiritual self. In the after-death state, such eventualities as heavenly realms and divine light are visible, but to merge with such rarified states we cannot merely grasp them. We are like novice swimmers, afraid to release our grip on the pier but desiring to swim to an enchanting island just out of reach. We let go of what we are holding on to, to reach for what is more alluring. We need to transform the inner self so that we are sufficiently unmoored of our former, material concerns, permitting ourselves to be spiritually transformed by death—this is the message I hear from the near-death experience. The near-death tale unfolds in vignettes, or stages, which tell us the story of spiritual surrender. On earth, surrender can take the form of glorious pomp and liturgy, or breathing celestial rhythms of chant and praise. Or we may prefer a threadbare, unvarnished form of worship. We may surrender our souls in meditative trance or in rejoicing over a savior. Our prayers may sprout amid the rocks of solitude or rise with an assembly of voices to the roof of a community soul—a church. We may share our surrender with many or we may isolate our surrender. The likes of Allah, Jesus, or Buddha may blaze in our eyes, or there may be no form for the divine that we accept. No path excludes the rest, nor, I believe, defines us spiritually apart from our brethren on this earth. All spirituality, when not polluted by self-conceits, is an acceptable conduit for surrender.

And what are we surrendering to? Unmistakably, we are told by near-death survivors that we are opening to unity and unjudging love, which is unity expressed. Albert Einstein was a mathematician of unity, looking for the great principle rather than the smallest possible cause. And in his scientific ventures he perceived a universe essentially lit from within—defined by light, not by a machine-works. This was reflected in his view that we must enjoin life, surrendering our solitary self-image to a circle of inclusion. For it is only from within this circle, he felt, that we can generate the compassion that will assure life's continuity in this perilous age. Einstein referred to our usual narcissism as an "optical delusion" which occurs when we believe that our own life has been set adrift from all else. He went on to say, "The delusion is a kind of prison for us, restricting us to our personal desires and to affection for just a few people nearest to us. Our task must be to free ourselves of this prison by widening our circle of compassion to embrace all living creatures and the whole of creation in its beauty." With these words, Einstein perfectly echoes what is at the heart of the near-death experience—a reunion, or return to unity. Within this brief pause in life, we are taught to begin to cultivate a sense of connectedness with the rest of life. And once this connection is made we naturally respond with compassion.

As we explore the spiritual interpretations of the near-death experience, it may seem that what the accounts tell us is too wonderful to be true. It may seem too much like a hidden miracle awaiting us in the most secret part of our lives. But I would urge readers to consider what Saint Augustine wrote on the subject in his *Confessions:*

> Miracles do not happen to us in contradiction to nature, but only in contradiction to that which is known to us of nature. *(Saint Augustine 1953)*

As we explore the sevenfold path of reunion in the near-death experience, we will be implored to spiritually engage life, to love compassionately and thereby transform ourselves. It is our task, then, to surrender to this transformation, a gesture which allows us to fully thrive in a non-material, spiritually resonant reality. A challenge awaits us which I believe to be the most joyous of all life's possibilities.

And so I offer this slim book as a handbook for death in the tradition of the medieval Christian work, *Ars Moriendi,* the Art of Dying. It is not my work really, but belongs to the many who have given foundation to it by permitting me to share in their near-death stories. It is with gratitude to them that I present this seven-fold overview of death in the hope that it may lead others upon the path of spiritual Reunion.

My Recollections of Death

I grew up in a shanty town in southern Ohio, my life only slightly removed from the poverty my family had brought with them to America and never quite managed to shed. I was the first born by six years. My father had worked as a laborer since he was a child, but for all his rugged strength, he was always gentle with me. I must have been a disappointment to him, for I was a quiet, sickly child, born into his family of rugged construction workers and coal miners.

We had little money for pleasures, but my father loved to take us night fishing whenever possible along the narrow, muddy banks of the Little Miami River. We would stay out until quite late, hunched over our cane poles in the hissing lantern light. On one of these trips, when I was no more than five years old, I fell into the water and almost drowned.

Of the rest of that night I have no memory. To begin with, we usually foraged for bait in a marshy area abutting the river. My father carved branches and drove them into the soft bank of the river. Resting our fishing poles on these fulcrums, we would then sit back and lazily watch the cork, a satellite of red and white, ride the river's murky waves. These rituals I remember well as the fabric of my young life. We would sit on the bank upon blankets, a cooler and kerosene lantern nearby. I would often explore the bank or the dark fringe of the woods, my fishing pole left for my mother to attend. Or I would sit and dreamily gaze across the water, listening to the strange stirring of night. Upon the night of my accident, my father decided to fish for a while beneath the bridge spanning the highway. I tried to follow him. The bank was composed of many sand bars which I ran blindly across in pursuit of my father.

Before I realized it, I had tripped and plunged into the dark river. I struggled only briefly, for I was stricken numb by the inrush of water. Each gasping breath seared my lungs. It was an agony I shall never forget. Then I immediately plummeted into a darkness in which my fear and agony vanished. In an instant I was outside the darkness, looking down upon the river from above, its surface like the glowing tungsten from our lantern, my father bent over the river's edge peering in. My father recalls plunging his arm into the water and drawing me out quickly. In contrast, I remember a slow unfolding of events which stood outside time. I could see very far and, in truth, was neither interested in my father nor considered my own fate. It all seemed very far away. Instead, I was mesmerized by the bird's-eye-view of the fading river as well as the last visible traces of sun upon the horizon. But what I remember most about my death was a resonating stillness, from within which everything I saw seemed to rise. It was rising within me as well, showing me that I belonged to it. It quietly hummed. Through it the stars were burning and the river flowed. And then I fell away from all sight and sound, and found myself inside that stillness.

I was pitched into a stillness so deep I could not think or act. For a while I just rested there, beyond all care. I merged with that mute emptiness and was no longer aware of having a mind of my own or even of still being alive. Yet it was not unpleasant; I was at ease beyond all possibilities and hopes. After a while, though I had no sense of the passage of time, I began to move. I began gracefully to spin about. I found myself performing a slow pirouette in that stillness. And then a light dawned, far away and above me. And as I turned I began rising toward it. I later imagined my ascent in a great many ways, but most often I pictured it as a whirling ladder, its rungs leading me toward an indescribably glorious light. It was as though the stillness or emptiness was winding around itself, forging a passage to light. That was all that was happening— the light and stillness, one giving way to the other. Yet the stillness was not being replaced by the light. Rather, the stillness was the primordial womb from which even the light itself arose. The motion I felt was stillness giving birth to light. Even then I recognized it as the dance of life.

The closer I was drawn to this brilliant light, the more it unveiled its essence, which I felt as love. It was an unjudging embrace of light that perfectly cherished and hoped for me, that cared for and empathized with all life. Exposed to this light, my self-image burned away. I was not a child; I was light perceiving itself in a mirror of light. All that was glorious or sacred about life shone from this light, just as all creative fires raged within it. It remains, these many years afterward, just as intensely memorized as it is hopelessly indescribable. All that I can really say of it is that, very briefly, I gazed into the light and found myself. I longed to stay in the light's embrace. And then my father reached into the river and saved me. With a great inrush, my life again compressed itself into a tiny, frail figure. Once again, I was alone and afraid, my lungs burning, my heart racing.

And after this brief death I only wanted to be left alone. I took no interest in the life I was supposed to be leading. I rebelled for many years against all efforts to instruct me in its necessities. Most often, I remained mute and stubbornly detached. I desperately wanted to return to the light and incessantly grieved being exiled from it. Yet, try as I might, I could not find my way back. This after-effect of my experience was that I was lost, unable to reclaim the light, and set apart from the rest of life by its indelible memory.

Slowly, I grew more attached to the world. After many years of enduring the jarring aftermath of my little death, including many maddening upheavals, I merely wanted to be included in the life I seemed to perpetually look upon from outside. Just prior to my teen years, I began to awkwardly throw myself into life's turmoil and pleasures. I sought to live as simply and materially as my peers, attracted to and filled with their pursuits and dreams. Beyond the light, I found many alluring visions, many hopes that had gone unnoticed until then. The world promised its own rewards, held its own fascinations, which I began to pursue. And unlike my love for the light, these rewards were understood by everyone.

I had always sketched, ever since I was able to hold a pencil. What finally put the light firmly behind me was my love for art. I imagined that I would eventually be a famous artist, my paintings exhibited in galleries the world over. When I was accepted because of my talent, the praise I received strengthened a bond with an as yet underdeveloped self-image which my vision of the light seemed to have held at bay. The more this self-image flourished, the farther away and more dreamlike my death in the river seemed. Finally, I looked upon the light as no more than a child's fantasy, a distracting self-indulgence I was glad to be rid of. Eventually, I so successfully suppressed the memory that it almost vanished entirely from my life. But I also found that I had sacrificed both my innocence and my spiritual self, and I grew increasingly more cynical—a perplexing reversal for my parents to witness. The child who had once been so quietly reserved and self-giving was suddenly rude and self-absorbed. If it had not been for the young girl whom I loved as I grew up, I probably would never have recovered. It was her faith in me, her struggle to redeem my heart, which undoubtedly made it possible to finally claim that vision. For I made no effort on my own behalf.

When I was eighteen, I enrolled in a Fine Arts program at a local university that had acquired its staff of teachers from New York City. I was planning to relocate to New York when college was finished so I was pleased to study with them. To earn tuition I began painting houses. While painting the house of an elderly nurse, who happened to be the director of a fledgling children's hospital, I was offered a job. I was hired on as an orderly in surgery to begin with, then was transferred to the emergency room shortly afterward. When school resumed, I began working the night shift so I could attend classes during the day.

Within a year of taking the job, an event occurred which again changed the direction of my life. While on duty one night, I was paged by a nurse to assist her in transporting a body to the morgue. The body was that of an emaciated young girl, no more than twelve. She had been beautiful once, before the illness had taken so much from her. Even a month earlier, I remembered her walking in the courtyard while leaning on her mother for support, her beauty only then beginning to grow dim. Replacing life's radiance now was the startling whiteness of her flesh, which seemed to burn away the darkness in the room. Her unfeeling fingers had a rosary tangled among them. Her child's features were quietly composed, as though she had found the perfect sleep. Her face betrayed no hint of her perpetual agony, but it was apparent that her body had been tortured down to the bone before death finally claimed her. I had never been so moved in my life; tears blurred my sight as I bent over to touch the unfeeling cold that had invaded her. The nurse looked at me pityingly but then went on with her work. I could not get over the fact that everything was gone, that everything she had hoped, longed for, dreamed of, had been utterly erased. She looked like a young girl, but within her there was only a purposeless vacancy.

As I busied myself with preparing the cart, memories of my own death, buried for so many years, awoke within me. With an almost unbearable clarity, I relived much of it, seeing the darkness pour over me again as I desperately struggled. It was as though I was helplessly sinking again—even my personality seemed to have vanished. I was emptied of all self, so that I felt like a husk which was as vacant as this child's body on the cart. I did not return to the light, nor did any of the spiritual aspects of my experience return to me. Rather, there was just a wrench-ing away of all my dreams and desires, so that when I finally arrived in the morgue and lifted the child to put her in a drawer, it was as though I was lifting myself as well. I was again sinking beneath the river, beyond all cares and hopes, unconcerned with art, with my life, with the many ambitions I had convinced myself were worth struggling for—I was desireless and empty.

For two days I was numb, neither attending art classes nor reporting to work. Sleeplessly, I paced the floors at night or sat mummified in blankets on the bed, vacantly staring into the darkness. There was no ethereal light, there was just the pitiless shadow of death upon me. All gestures of hope or love had been abandoned—I was bitterly numb within. Death would always be waiting to swallow our entire life, leaving no trace. Life was meaningless folly. I was so stricken by this meaninglessness that I had no desire to go on living. Weak and resigned to my fate, I sat alone in my apartment.

Death was constantly with me, its shadow engulfing my life. I wished I had drowned that evening in the river; then I would not be enduring this torment. I would have passed out of exis-tence as a child, the nothingness taking away life's incurable wounds. Death had so effectively exiled me from life that I barely noticed what was happening to me, and cared even less. Whenever I tried to sleep, there was a sense of this emptiness pouring into me, exchanging my sense of self with a barren void. I struggled against this, still vainly holding on to life. So I paced the floors, mumbling madly to myself. Finally, I grew too weak to continue my vigil and decided to give in and per-mit this emptiness to have its way. I would lie down and sur-render to it, and if death resulted then I much preferred it to this ordeal.

I struggled into bed, stretching stiffly out. I saw many things all at once, such as the child sliding into the morgue drawer, my father's face when he pulled me from the river, his eyes so softly afraid. I had felt the river rising up around me. I sank into that emptiness, far from my body. I could even hear my own thoughts, which seemed to go on without me. As I descended into the emptiness, these thoughts grew fainter until finally there was no trace of them remaining. Yet this emptiness was not merely vacant and still. What I had perceived as an emptiness was also a fullness; an intense energy not yet shaped.

But then I felt a far-away trembling. I realized it was my own body, pulsing tremendously with energy. It was as though my body was a tuning fork vibrating more and more rapidly. The body's fabric seemed to be tearing apart, the energy so rapidly pulsating that it finally grew fiery, as though I was about to incinerate from within. Just at the crucial instant, when it seemed apparent that my body could endure no more of this force, I was thrown out of my body. I was rushing through an invisible space at an unimaginable speed. I was rising so quickly that I had no sense of light or darkness, time or timelessness. All that I was aware of was an overwhelming bliss which was so intense that no pleasure life had to offer could even remotely compare with it. I realized as well that this was death. Any more that I would say about the experience would be misleading, except that it was both incomparably beautiful and fierce.

Then I grew aware that I was approaching the light of God. Not the God we usually conceive of, but a being more inexhaustibly benevolent and awake, wiser and mightier than any God I could dare imagine. I was steadily being drawn into the light while thoroughly inebriated by the magnificence of it. There was a wordless communication, an invitation to join with Him in the light. I was overjoyed. When I reached the brink of merging with that sunlike brilliance, a sudden thought occurred to me. It was quite unexpected and for very many years had been forgotten. I remembered that after my brush with death in the river, my mother had remarked it would be almost unbearable for her to outlive one of her children. It was the only calamity in life she prayed to God to be spared. As soon as this thought occurred I was thrown back into my bed.

Within a few months I had two more death experiences, one of which seemed to show the way I had died in a former life and what had taken place long afterward. What I experienced went far beyond the usual near-death experience. It was similar to the post-mortem states described in the *Tibetan Book of the Dead*, which lead to a rebirth. I finally entered a state where I grew so afraid that I lost all control and was carried helplessly along by powerful energies. It was a lesson to me that fear can provoke the most severe consequences in the after-death states. I also realized, in the third near-death experience, that love powerfully counteracts any negative after-death state. By resorting to love rather than fear, I was also finally able to surrender to and benefit from the final death experience. It was apparent that if love rules death, then it must also rule over life. Without love, the negative aspects of both life and death are unredeemable. We become truly lost.

Another result of these three near-death experiences was that I began having frequent out-of-body journeys. Almost every night when I lay down, the vibrations would return, separating me from my physical body at the brink of sleep. Along with the vibration, I would hear discordant, grating sounds, see flashes of light, and then would be outside my sleeping form, outside physical reality altogether. I would be floating in my room yet untouchably removed from its physical nature. I could see and think but I had no form. My movements were not restricted by physical objects. I passed through walls, moving with the speed of thought wherever I desired.

Whatever the objective reality of such states, they were mine to deal with. They rose often and entirely of their own accord. My near-death experience had, from an apparently cellular root, changed the way I viewed and lived reality. Touching death, I discovered, reorients our lives, often in ways we would not have invited or expected. I firmly believe in the realities that arose as a result of my experience, but in turn look upon such beliefs as unnecessary. They are part of the three unanswerable riddles posed to Buddha by a novice monk. As you proceed in this book, such experiences can just as easily be read metaphorically. All the pictorial language of the near-death experience can be interpreted as symbolism for reunion, looked upon as imaginatively generated forms that arise on the threshold of the return of our elements to their physical matrix. Perhaps they are just nature's way of throwing the doors of the psyche wide to the cosmos as it in turn flows in. I prefer to see these images as a pathway to transcendence—personally, I have gathered too much evidence to view it otherwise—death is what life has yet to imagine about itself. In this enterprise, out-of-body travel and spiritual energies are mere pointers which do not have to be glorified. Like all else in the spiritual life, the only proper response is to accept such phenomena, looking upon them as a refiner's fire bringing us closer to unity and love.

What Is the Near-Death Experience?

Using near-death tales as resources, the stages of death have been described since ancient ages. Fragments of near-death reports surface in the Bible alluding to a state of blessedness after death. In Genesis, Jacob has a dream which is startlingly like many later near-death accounts. Jacob lies down in the wilderness, his only pillow a stone, and has a dream. In the dream he envisions a ladder, its roots planted in the earth, its crown extending into heaven itself. Upon this ladder are angels, apparently using it as a bridge from heaven to earth. Then God appears to him, promising that his descendants will be as "plentiful as the dust on the ground."

Within Jewish, Christian, and Islamic sources are many accounts of saints journeying to the heavens and the throne of God, their ascent giving them the authority to preach or prophesy. Plato described an ancient near-death motif in his legend of "Er" in *The Republic*, a tale about the soul's journey into postmortal regions borrowed from unnamed Orphic and Pythagorean sources, which in turn probably were brought West from India. In the culminating event of *The Republic*, a link between the death mythologies of East and West was forged. Plato's view of the universe was three-tiered, beginning with a lower, sensory realm, then rising to an etheric plateau of spirits, gods, and demons. Finally, there was the pure Beyond, which he envisioned as a realm of ideas leading to the pure, divine Light. Though evidence of this phenomenon dates back to archaic cultures, visionary near-death reports were common in medieval cultures the earth over. In the sixth century, many near-death tales were recorded in the *Dialogues* of Pope Gregory I, who also ordered the sacred hymns to be preserved and catalogued which afterward flourished as Gregorian chant. His death stories, though, are weighted heavily toward proving an afterlife and postmortem accountability—for which we must depend on the church as intercessionist. The Venerable Bede of the eighth century recorded the tale of a Northumbrian man who died and inexplicably returned to life during last rites, sitting straight up in bed. He reported that he had met a figure "of shining countenance" who led him on a tour of the over- and under-worlds of death; in this journey he was given a taste of the divine light and bliss of heaven. He spent the rest of his life in the effort to retrace his steps to heaven, ridding himself of all possessions and entering a monastery. Touring the heavens, or hells, under the watchful but loving eye of a being of light is still one of the most widely reported elements of the near-death experience. Such figures of light are described in the Gospels as ushering in the resurrection at the tomb of Jesus. Mohammed journeyed through the heavens on a white steed, a figure of light whom he identified as the archangel Gabriel serving as his guide leading him finally to the throne of God—a journey which sanctioned him as the final prophet of Islam. Surviving artwork from various ages and regions of the earth portray similar journeys and spiritual rebirths.

The near-death experience has illuminated the shadow regions of life for ages, transmuting the poisons of death into a divine ambrosia. It has spoken, as it still speaks, of the journey hidden within consciousness. It seems to tell the truer story we all share, the story which is the kernel within the shell of life. Even though a medieval monk may have interpreted it quite differently from a pagan goat-herder or a modern Hasidic, when you examine their near-death stories, they remain essentially consistent. We live in a fortunate age, for these accounts, once isolated from one another, have been drawn together into the first-ever overview of the near-death tale. This is due to both the advent of modern resuscitative arts and the melding of the world's cultures after so many fragmentary ages. This pause, this half step between life and death, is being looked at anew in every culture on earth. Numberless voices have testified, giving us an exhaustive account of what it is like to die.

Near-death events have often redefined history, as many of the revelations of the great religions occurred on the cusp between life and death. Buddha was famished, near death, when he conceived the "Middle Way," the pillar upon which was erected the Buddhist religion. When Saint Paul was thrown from a horse and struck senseless, he saw the holy light that made him a follower of Jesus, a conversion that redefined the entire Western world. Saint Augustine recorded the report of a physician who was gripped by the fear of death and plunged into a crisis of faith—as a result he had two near-death experiences, which told him many things about life after death as well as restoring his faith in God. The *Egyptian Book of the Dead* is a manual for dying, composed when Egypt was at its imperial height. And the *Tibetan Book of the Dead* is undoubtedly the most exhaustive account ever composed on what happens after death and how to negotiate the transition from life into death. The book itself, as legend would have it, is a *terma*, or hidden treasure discovered by a spiritual pilgrim in a mountain cave in southern Tibet many years after it was originally written. Since its discovery, it has not only been studiously memorized by Buddhist monks but has also been recited in the ear of many thousands of dying souls.

Native American shamans such as Black Elk have been chosen as spiritual elders by virtue of their near-death adventures. They have presided over tribal death down through the ages and still do in many remote regions of the earth. A shaman is trained in the art of dying, either literally or figuratively.

Shamans such as Black Elk are often recognized as children, when they return from fevers or encounters with death with tales of divine visions. If they do not receive their calling naturally, many shamans seek it out, putting their life at risk in an effort to fertilize their spiritual life with a death vision. Candidates often subject themselves to deprivation and isolation in the wilderness in search of such a vision.

The near-death report is a collective vision of death. The many stages of the near-death event might more appropriately be referred to as realms, for witnesses actually find themselves in a distinct setting during each stage. No one person is known to have gone through every stage in the near-death experience, but by collecting the myriad testimonies, a single near-death model has emerged. This model reveals the near-death experience to be a progressive, unfolding event which strips away all life and then spiritually recreates it. The earliest stages in the model are usually of an ineffable nature, such as immersion in light. The light then unfolds to reveal many stages which define for us more recognizable spiritual acts such as surrender, faith, and love. Within each stage a transformation is initiated, as the person is repeatedly reshaped. The person's identity is spiritually distilled, remade, until the last stage—a return to the body—where these transformations can finally be translated into a life's work. This stage may be the most crucial of all.

Light defines the near-death experience, as both the visions of the dying person and their consciousness itself seem to be illuminated. Light voicelessly expresses to the dying person an unequivocal love for all existence. It is described as the essence, as the beating heart of life, revealed finally at death. I tend to view the near-death experience as the spiritual equivalent of Einstein's theory of light. Life was spiritually redefined by the near-death experience shortly after Einstein materially redefined it. Within all the intricacies of our universe, there is just light and more light, always wonderfully perfect. Einstein discovered light at the farthest edge of the universe; the near-death narrators have found light at the farthest edge of life itself, beyond the visible universe.

There are also many direct teachings to be found within the near-death experience, when people find themselves before a being of light. This being is the personification of the light. From this being, near-death survivors have learned there is always a spiritual path before them, both during life and after death. They are encouraged to mature spiritually, learning to surrender and love. Both in words and wordlessly, they are informed of an underlying unity to all life—every aspect of existence is revealed as deeply interwoven and interconnected. This is what the Buddhist sage Thich Nhat Hanh has referred to as "interbeing." Love is the indivisible force of life as it flows from its unmanifest source into the field of manifestation and time. At death, this flow is merely reversed as life flows toward the source rather than away from it. During the near-death experience this force is revealed—love is visible as light. Love is that which mends life's visible and invisible rifts.

Most people return from the near-death experience with a belief in reincarnation, even though fewer than a third considered it before. The regeneration of personal life is strikingly apparent to most near-death experiencers, even among children raised with conflicting beliefs. Yet a belief in reincarnation is not necessary to appreciate the validity of the near-death experience and what it teaches.

Advances in the field of medicine have made the near-death experience much more prevalent, so that the science that would most often refute such a mystical concept is exactly what has enabled it to flourish. The near-death experience does not refute science's view of the universe, it just addresses a different reality. As a result, we are learning that mysticism is just as pressing a necessity as science. Mysticism is the irrational self put in order, just as science is the rational self put in order. Both the rational and irrational irrefutably exist, the twin polarities of the psyche. It seems apparent as well that both need to be equally addressed. Subjects undergoing surgery have had near-death experiences despite the fact that monitors have shown no brain activity during their "death". Even when the brain waves measured by science have vanished, it seems the mystic in us continues on. The electrical activity of the brain may not be responsible for mysticism, it may well be a distinct reality.

Most near-death experiences occur when the most vital of organs, the endlessly plodding heart, is stilled. A few have been reported by individuals after comas, a death-like state in which only the most rudimentary signs of life remain, the brain itself barely functioning. There have also been near-death accounts given by people so terrorized or stressed that they were sure they were dying. Struck overboard during a sailing accident, a friend of mine had such a near-death experience; his momentary unconsciousness resulted in a vivid near-death scene. Often, such near-death events require only that life is in peril for them to arise. Letting go of our inner self seems to be as essential to having a near-death experience as actual cessation of physical life signs. Anyone who has worked with the seriously ill has met with people who have just "let go" of life. Often, they have been stable for weeks, yet they announce that they are "ready". Afterward they go quickly, often that very night. They behave as though they have seen into death and have abandoned any fear. These events give evidence of hidden latches that hold consciousness in the body, which can be released by any manner of events, most notably physical death itself. And there is further evidence that once these latches have been released, it is much more likely the experience can be repeated.

Only about a third of those revived from a death episode report a near-death experience. The experience, I believe, may simply be untranslatable and so goes unremembered. The physicist Jacob Bohm has likened this process to an enfolding of consciousness. As you rise into a subtler, more psychic reality, there is an *un*folding or expansion of consciousness; but as you fall again into a grosser, more physical reality, that psychic reality again *en*folds—it vanishes from our awareness.

This may perhaps be more clearly explained by the Biblical image of Jacob's ladder, which bridges heaven to earth. The rungs of Jacob's ladder could be looked upon as a hierarchy of reality, higher rungs representing progressively more "heavenly" or celestial realms, lower rungs representing more earthly existence. The ladder is perceived at first to be invisible, except for the first, most earth-bound rung. As you ascend, rungs appear one by one, the one above still unseen, the lower ones remaining visible. The reverse is true as you descend, the rungs vanish one by one. The ladder unfolds to the extent you ascend and enfolds to the extent you descend. So climbing up and down the ladder, your individual reality, or consciousness, expands or contracts.

In the near-death experience, we are simply rising upon the rungs of the ladder, then descending toward the physical solidity we briefly abandoned. Whether or not we remember and are transformed by the experience, then, depends upon how fully we identify with our subtler, more psychic reality. It is, as we will see, a matter of surrender. This model remains accurate, I think, regardless of whether you believe the near-death experience to be strictly psychological and physical in nature or whether you view it as transcendent.

Because of the ineffability of the rungs, near-death experiencers repeatedly warn us that speech is inadequate to describe these remarkable transitions. Even those with vivid recollections are often aware of aspects of the event that are irretrievable, or again enfold when they return to their body. Often, they are even aware of realizations that promptly vanished once they returned. This erasure of memory can be unfortunate; it is my firm belief that the more vividly we retain the image of our own death, the more intensely our lives are transformed. But nevertheless, such brushes with death almost always serve to amplify life's finest qualities, giving it a profundity which it often lacks otherwise.

According to Plato, death is merely the loosening of the restrictions on life and the freeing of its essence. We simply let go of our familiar life and surrender to a life we have not yet imagined. It is a wondrous, even perilous journey, like that of Odysseus, in which we undergo trials of the spirit. While upon his deathbed, Plato was asked by a visitor to summarize his life's work in a single phrase. Without hesitation, Plato replied, "practicing for death." I would like to suggest that we weave this sentiment into our lives, joining our view of life with death. Unlike Plato, we have the advantage of a vast collection of near-death literature and thousands of personal stories to guide us. This modern day overview of death renders this task less imposing than it was in Plato's day.

— —

There is an old story about two travelers upon a steep path leading across the Himalayas. The travelers happen to be the devil and a recent convert of his, both wearing a pilgrim's disguise. Directly ahead of them on the treacherous path, a yogi emerges from a cave where he has resided in solitude for uncountable years. He is radiant to behold, the illumination gained through many years of spiritual discipline visibly manifesting itself. It is spiritually uplifting, even to the devil, to look upon him. The newly realized saint reaches into his robe and draws from his heart a spiritual jewel.

> The devil's servant: "Isn't that truth he just found in his heart?"
> "Yes, yes it is," replies the devil casually.
> "Well isn't that bad business for you?" his companion inquires.
> "Not at all," replies the devil. "I'm going to help him organize it."

Spiritual jewels litter our inner life, rarely even glanced at. When we meet with such a treasure, we usually set it apart from the rest of our life, burying it among the litany of religious doctrines that belong to our particular culture. Most of the precious spiritual jewels in our keeping have been overlain with many layers of dogma, until they are finally hidden beneath the doctrines originally meant to protect them. The near-death experience is a universal realization that does not belong to any one religion. And unlike the ancient texts on death, such as the *Tibetan Book of the Dead*, it has not arisen among sages in the wilderness. It addresses our hearts because it is born among the struggles of civilization. It does not exclusively reflect or exclude the views of any of the earth's cosmologies, but belongs to them all.

If you listen carefully to the near-death experiencers' tales, you will hear the refrain—at the heart of all religion is personal experience and faith. The Sanskrit word for faith is *visvas*. Its translation is wonderfully simple: "to breathe easily." It tells us to invest our lives with a trust that makes it so easy to accept our own spiritual nature that we can breathe easily, free of fear for our future. This is a wonderful sentiment with which to begin our spiritual life, and it is likely that its sweetness will continue to nourish. All spiritual nourishment seems to enter us through a sense of faith or trust. Without this ability "to breathe easily," we cannot feel secure enough to surrender to an inner, higher reality.

Such faith arises directly from trusting and accepting our own innermost nature. Trust grows when we begin to sharpen our inner vision, taking on a more secure sense of self. The legacy of the saints and sages is that we turn our vision around, looking at where consciousness and our sense of identity arise from. "Mysticism" and "mystery" are derived from the same Greek root word, *muein*, which means closing the eyes or mouth—suggesting that we shut the doors of the senses. Implicit in the mysticism of this earth is the practice of cultivating trances or shifts in attention, which have more in common with sleep or death than our usual waking state. Even though we all sleep and dream, as we shift away from familiar landmarks, consciousness usually begins to vanish. The only difference with the mystic is he strives to remain aware during these shifts of consciousness—he takes his conscious self with him. In the jargon of mysticism—he meditates. To meditate then is simply to self-mediate our own shifts of consciousness rather than passively letting them happen to us. As the near-death event relentlessly reminds us, the heart of this venture is an inner unfolding, possible only when it is consciously submitted to. It cannot affect our habitual, waking self except through self-surrender; only by refusing to leave behind our waking self can we reunify with the more potent, spiritually resonant depths of our own nature. So self-surrender is also, paradoxically, self-growth and the expansion of our consciousness.

But it requires deep faith to close the doors and expectantly wait. To shut our eyes and wait makes us vulnerable not only to what is outside us but perhaps even more so to what awaits within. This is what the near-death experience relays to us as well—to trust in the divine implies that it is always already with us, that it is very close. And we cannot be any closer to the divine than sharing with it our innermost self. So the near-death experience teaches us to trust and feel secure in a divine nature untouched and untroubled by changing events.

There are many ways of surrendering to the divine. The most popular on earth is worship of a divine image which our faith is unshakably attached to, such as Christ in the West or Krishna in the East. Often, it is envisioned as a love affair with this icon, most often an amalgam of many spiritually resonant myths and legends. The worshiper is then drawn away from himself toward this divine image, which is also a symbol for his own spiritual self. The worshiper surrenders outwardly and opens inwardly, his love pouring his consciousness back into his own depths. The result is that he falls in love with the divine.

There are no superior or inferior forms of inner surrender. Many people are drawn to either mystical or rational surrender, others to a more devotional approach. All spiritual life depends on successive surrenders to a divine reality underlying the material one. It is these successive surrenders, these possibilities, which the near-death experience defines, I believe, better than any spiritual document ever written. And they each depend equally on our passionate spiritual nature to succeed. Quite simply, we bare our souls through passionately yearning for the divine, whether our approach is quietly meditative or passionately devotional. To yearn for the divine is also to trust our own hearts, which is where divinity is concealed in what has often been described as a bittersweet game of hide and seek.

It has been found that it is difficult to intentionally have a near-death experience. Being well-versed in near-death lore does not make it more likely to happen, and there is even evidence that it prevents it, very likely because the experience itself has become the desired object of spiritual gain. Spiritual transformation, the sages often remind us, depends not upon beholding mystical wonders but on transcending the boundaries of our personal self to realize the unity and love underlying all of life. We have all glimpsed this unity. Many find this in churches, others in the temples of art or science. Often, it is inspired by no more than a sunlit lake, a wreath of mist, the roar of the surf—which seem to reverberate infinitely within us, unspeakably sacred and glorious. For in instant, we flow out of ourselves into a unified field of life.

Personally, I have always found that fulfillment arises when I give of myself and serve others. And it has been most helpful to judge my spiritual progress not by what I experience but by what I am able to share of myself and the efficacy of what I have given. The near-death experience has served as a constant reminder to me of the inseparability of life and love. It is perhaps most beneficial to read the near-death experience as a way to rid ourselves of doubts concerning the virtue of love and self-giving. This may be its simplest and yet most profound message.

In the next chapter, we will begin to explore the spiritual treasures distilled throughout the stages in the near-death experience. It is my hope that this dialogue will inspire you to spiritually prepare for death. Many people, when terminally ill and face-to-face with death, express regret at having neglected their spiritual life. There is a feeling of incompleteness or of having compromised their most cherished beliefs. I believe that regardless of a belief in God or an afterlife, each of us possesses a spiritual vision. If, as death draws in upon us, we have not realized that vision and have left unexplored the themes of unity and love, we may be left with the hollow feeling that it is too late. For the purpose of reclaiming our spiritual impulses, I have devised from the near-death experience a spiritual map; its many elements a transcendent cartography. The following seven stages will be familiar to those readers well-versed in the literature of near-death. But I redivided them in an effort to enhance their spiritual clarity and accessibility:

The Seven Stages of Spiritual Reunion:

I. **Separation from the physical body.** We find ourself outside the physical body, often seeing it from a slight distance. The mind is not only intact, but it seems to be greater, wiser, and more powerful. Often the person describes inhabiting a cloud of energy or a field of light.

II. **The sacred emptiness.** We merge with a stillness and emptiness which fills us with unimaginable peace.

III. **Immersion in light and love.** There may be a sense of rising through a tunnel. Or the light may just break and overwhelm us. It is most often described as the most beautiful sight imaginable. We are made aware of having met with the *source* of all light and all love.

IV. **The light personified.** When we draw near to the light, it usually takes on a holy form—a saint, savior, or spiritual sage with whom we are most at ease. The light then is able to teach, becoming the personification of love and wisdom. Great joy arises from the meeting with the being of light and we are instilled with the rarified spiritual qualities we have been estranged from, especially unqualified love.

V. **Spirits as benefactors and guides.** During this stage of the near-death experience, most people discover that during both life and in death they are given guidance by spiritual beings. The primary duty of these angel-like spirits seems to be either to deliver us to the light or to teach us how to prepare ourselves so that we can learn from the things we have done and thereby progress spiritually.

VI. **A panoramic life review.** We see the deeds of our life through the eyes of everyone we have ever given love to or withheld love from. The vision is not merely a series of images but is actually lived, emotions felt.

VII. **A return to life and transformation.** A boundary is sensed or pictured which tells us we can go no further. At this point, we are often allowed to decide whether or not to go on or return to our former body.

Stage One: Separation from the Physical Body

The first stage of the near-death experience is marked by a reversal of the subject's most cherished beliefs about reality. The sense of self is turned inside out, suddenly existing outside physical reality. We observe our physical body from outside it, usually from an elevated viewpoint. Accounts abound of the deceased looking on as physicians and caregivers strive to resuscitate the body. This aspect of the near-death experience is most accessible to research and is its only verifiable element. Many people who have had such an experience have later described very detailed scenes and events they could not have otherwise witnessed. In the seminal work, *Life after Life,* a woman described the first stage of the near-death experience in this way:

> Just then I heard the nurses shout, "Code pink! Code Pink!" As they were saying this, I could feel myself moving out of my body and sliding down between the mattress and the rail on the side of the bed—actually it seemed as if I went through the rail—on down to the floor. Then, I started rising upward, slowly. On my way up, I saw more nurses come running into the room—there must have been a dozen of them. My doctor happened to be making rounds in the hospital, so they called him, and I saw him come in, too. I thought, "I wonder what he's doing here."

I drifted on past the light fixture—I saw it from the side and very distinctly—and then I stopped, floating right below the ceiling, looking down…

I watched them reviving me from up there! My body was lying down there stretched out on the bed, in plain view, and they were all standing around it. I heard one nurse say, "Oh my God! She's gone!" while another one leaned down to give me mouth-to-mouth resuscitation. I was looking at the back of her head while she was doing this…

As I saw them below, beating on my chest and rubbing my arms and legs, I thought, "Why are they going to so much trouble? I'm just fine now." *(Moody 1975)*

During the out-of-body experience, you subjectively realize you were never a physical being. Having shed your physical density, you discover an immutably richer, vaster, and more creatively potent life. Freed of former restraints, your mind is swift and powerful. The sense of sight is gloriously vivid, able to perceive at any distance. Within your mind is an imaginative fire, so that wherever you wish to travel you immediately arrive, and whatever you desire for yourself immediately manifests. In this stage, when the mind first emerges from its restraints, it has often been compared to a butterfly emerging from a cocoon. In her autobiography, Elizabeth Kubler-Ross recounts her visit to prison wards of gutted Nazi concentration camps just after World War II, where she saw many lovingly drawn portraits of butterflies, an ancient symbol for alchemical transformation. During the near-death experience, a subtler, more spiritual self emerges from within us, baptized in its own inner energies and grown immeasurably more powerful. As a symbol of this transition the butterfly's array of colors serves well, for the mental body emerging at death is often described as a luminous rainbow of energies. Just as recognized as a ritual symbol for this transformation is the snake, which sheds its outer skin, giving birth to a youthful, replenished self.

After this transformation, near-death survivors most often feel little affinity for the physical corpse, which looks to be no more than a mirage-like after-image of a life they are glad to be rid of. Usually floating within view of the staff's labors to revive them, they express little interest in the affair, looking upon it with a dispossessed equanimity. There is usually little sorrow for the life just abandoned, but concern is expressed for the staff's stressful efforts, which to the just-deceased often look absurd.

Among the spiritual tales of the Upanishads of India, this stage is referred to as the shedding of the physical sheath. Our true spirit is said to be enfolded within several perishable sheaths, each of which we identify with a self. As we remove each successive sheath, we grow more "liberated," a term which echoes through the religions of Asia. And what are we liberated from? From any self that is subject to death and so is less than our eternal identity. Mortal life is then viewed as a necessary refinery where our spiritual efforts burn away the dross of these unwanted identities. When at death we shed the bundle of cocoons that hide our eternal self, it is possible for us to be liberated—we are released from all illusions regarding our true nature. Or in theistic terms, when all the sheaths are taken away, it is possible to merge again with God. But liberation is not a *loss* of self, as many might fear, but the *regaining* of a self immeasurably more vast and powerful than we ever imagined.

When we move out of the physical body, waves of unseen forces are reported which can be heard, seen, or felt. We do not necessarily move away from the material word, but the range of our experience expands. Our former world is seen to be afloat within a much greater and more vibrant non-material world. The most noticeable element of this world is actually that it internally vibrates more rapidly, which is apparently what gives it its power. At this stage, near-death experiencers typically assert that only their brains and eyes remain, so that the essence of their mental power is intact while the grosser senses fall away. The mind reigns supreme in this stage, so that whatever we desire materializes. Energies flow with the mind, so there is no gap between what we imagine and what exists—we are powerful creators. Realities are intricately interwoven with our own minds, as we are constantly able to alter our reality with our thoughts and are lucidly aware of the thoughts of others. A Vietnam veteran described being in this state in *Recollections of Death*:

> I felt like I could have thought myself anywhere I wanted to be instantly…I just felt exhilarated with a sense of power. I could do whatever I wanted to…It's realer than here, really…
>
> I remember all of a sudden going right back to the battlefield where I had been lost…It was almost like you materialize there and all of a sudden the next instant you were over here. It was just like you blinked your eyes. *(Sabom 1982)*

He also explained that he was able to communicate directly with the minds of others:

> The thirteen guys that had been killed the day before that I had put in plastic bags were right there with me. And more than that, during the course of the month of May, my particular company lost forty-two dead. All forty-two of the guys were there. They were not there in the form we perceive the human body…But I knew they were there. I felt their presence. We communicated without talking with our voices. *(Sabom 1982)*

In Buddhism, this mental body has been referred to as a "wish-fulfilling gem," able to grant us any boon. In many cultures, this indwelling spirit has many names, but it is often identified by the newly deceased as a soul. A goal of many religions is merely to hold on to this mental body after death, for it has the ability to create paradises and dwell in heavens. In this state, the mind has access to unrestricted energy, which, according to the *Tibetan Book of the Dead,* can also be a curse. For if we have no spiritual moorings, the mind can also become lost in the labyrinth of emerging desires. So like all great powers, it is also rife with potential dangers. When we encounter myths regarding celestial paradises, I would think it likely that we are also hearing the echoes of ancient near-death experiences.

Tales of the discovery of this mental body abound in history. In her many raptures, Saint Teresa reported often journeying out-of-body, where she was "able to see with the eyes of her spirit much more clearly than she was able to see with the eyes of her body." While suffering a heart attack, psychologist Carl Jung reported separating from his physical body, after which he described himself as being surrounded by a "bright glow." Like all else within this mental realm, our body is like a subtle mercury. Many have testified to inhabiting a body of light or energy that assumes many shapes, transmuting into a shapeless radiance or even perfect versions of their mortal body. Our thoughts have no limits in this state and are capable of quickly transforming our reality. If we are not adequately prepared, our latent desires and tendencies can begin to govern us. We can unexpectedly grow wild or wrathful, meek or terrified, as our thoughts manifest themselves. Wherever our thoughts go in this in-between state, energies go as well. But because we are often not aware of our own thoughts, in this state we can easily become lost amid the rising forms of our own minds. This malady was described by such figures as Buddha as the tendency to think without being fully aware. We let our thoughts roam without consciously directing them; rather, they direct us. There are two fundamental cures for this malady, which has been diagnosed by every spiritual mysticism on earth. The first cure is to learn to surrender the mind itself by meditating on the quiet depths of consciousness beneath thought. This consists of gradually re-identifying with quieter but more potent depths of consciousness, which are also capable of ruling our minds. Meditation is the bitter-at-first medicine we must take to regain spiritual soundness, often requiring many years of diligent effort. The second cure is much easier. To apply this remedy, we make of our minds spiritual refineries, filling them to the brim with spiritual love by giving our minds over to such antidotes as prayer, praise, chant, and celebration. When our desires are spiritualized, our thoughts spontaneously give birth to spiritual realities in the afterlife. Neither of these remedies is mutually exclusive and both depend on a heartfelt surrender.

Out-of-body journeys have been cultivated in regions all over the earth for more than a millennium. Prehistorical shamanistic ritual and art describe such journeys, as does the most ancient yoga manual in existence, *The Yoga Sutras of Pantanjali*. Almost all spiritual literature on earth touches upon these journeys, many even proposing ways to invoke them. Pantanjali viewed this power of disembodied travel rather skeptically, as relatively easy to acquire but with no spiritual profundity. Socrates based his philosophy on this mental reality when he discussed "a world of ideas." He viewed our world as the physical translation of this mental world. Italian priest Alonzo de Liguiri often traveled out of body while starving to death in his prison cell in the late 1700s. The most remarkable of his journeys was seen by many witnesses when his apparition appeared at the deathbed of Pope Clement I.

Such experiences are very much a part of life. The out-of-body experience frequently occurs outside the bounds of the near-death experience and is the most commonly reported of all psychic events. About one person in twenty has claimed having a near-death experience, but as many as one in five has reported an out-of-body experience. There are many who apparently have a gift for leaving their body, especially in the early stages of sleep. Personally, I have gone on many such journeys, which began shortly after my death experiences in my late teens. Many out-of-body travelers have compiled journals, describing not only their adventures but providing us with glimpses of that mental, energy world. There is even evidence to suggest we all have out-of-body journeys each night, hidden within the imagery of our dreams. I have a friend whose out-of-body journeys began with him dreaming he was the pilot of a plane. As the dream continued, segments of the plane were sheared away until he was alone and flying. His personal imagery had given way to a recognizable out-of-body journey.

But it has also been my experience that an out-of-body journey is not the same as a near-death experience, though many hold the opposite view. I discovered a crucial difference between these two states over the years. Both states begin as an out-of-body journey, but in the near-death experience a series of events begins to unfold rapidly over which we have no control. This is when the classically definable near-death stages begin to arise, whereas the out-of-body traveler never moves past this first stage of death, his physical identity still remaining in charge of his mental one. As death unfolds, the near-death experiencer has no control over events but is compelled to go through the stages of death. The traces of your past identity remain with you, so you still can think and still have a self to relate to. Yet he also begins to realize there are much subtler powers at work which the self must either surrender to or resist as death unfolds, stage after stage. Liberation is not born of regaining control but of surrendering the self that desires control for a deathless self-identity.

Stage Two: Experiencing the Void

In *Closer to the Light*, a child of nine who had just fallen into the ocean and was not recovered for nine minutes describes the second stage of the near-death experience in this way:

> I felt absolutely nothing, not the water, not the sand, nothing. I was surrounded by silence, but wasn't afraid. I wanted to stay there forever. I have never since experienced such a feeling of peace. *(Morse and Perry 1990)*

In this stage, it is as though all of existence has been extinguished except the bare awareness of being alive. Apart from this consciousness there is no sensible universe. What has happened? The *Tibetan Book of the Dead* describes this as the inner death, when the subtle forces of the mind are transiently stilled; these psychic forces gathering in motionless unity just prior to ejecting from the body. The first stage is referred to as the outer dissolution, when the physical body perishes. In this second stage, the inner dissolution occurs as the forces that composed the psyche are first gathered, stilled, then in a rising torrent, permanently exit the body. In the first stage, a physical death occurred, whereas in this stage a mental death is enacted.

Many near-death experiencers have been aware that this stage represents a mental separation, and in the literature it has been frequently referred to as the point when "the ribbons are cut". In this stage, the psyche or mental life itself is translated into death. According to Tibetan death lore a rare opportunity is presented. Because all the energies are gathered and still, we are able to experience our consciousness in its most whole and undiluted state. Mystical literature the earth over describes this state in a variety of terms: Nirvana, the Self, God, Yahweh, Buddha Mind, Tao, Sunyata, Brahman. This state is not just a nothingness but everything reconciled. All opposites are at rest in this state, their embrace resulting in a forceful quiet, simultaneously both empty and full, still and forceful.

Very briefly during this second stage of the near-death experience, the individual mind is reunited with its source—the consciousness that illuminates mind. For a while, awareness is only aware of itself, until the forces responsible for the mind begin to stir again in the next stage. Because there is no imagery, most near-death witnesses refer to this state as an emptiness, which is usually not perceived as significant. Often, they envision themselves as briefly fading away, sinking into darkness, or growing inexplicably silent. Or they may just lapse into a brief sleep, this stage going unnoticed. Yet as the mystical Persian poet Jal al-Din Rumi once reminded listeners, "When you look at this innermost self what you see is the universe not yet created." *(Barks 1991)* It is not really emptiness, but the state of infinite potential from which all life springs. In Biblical language, it is the darkness prior to creation. But Rumi, as well as other lovers of life, passionately fused this unspeakable reality to the rest of his life, after which he inexhaustibly sang and danced around its invisible axis. "Why do you weep?" Rumi once cried, "The source is within you, and the entire world is springing from it. The source is full, and its water ever-flowing. Do not grieve, drink your fill." *(Barks 1991)* A mystic such as Rumi dwells on this earth while intoxicated with these ineffable waters, translating his inner unity into loving gestures and self-abandoning worship of God.

After Mother Teresa, the patron saint of the neglected and

forgotten, fused her life to the divine, the rest of her life became a ceaseless outpouring of benevolence and love. Her love, as does all genuine love, arose from a recognition of this same inner unity. As she herself described this transition from inner, silent unity to outer, manifest unity:

> Silence of the heart is necessary so that you can hear God everywhere—in the closing of the door, in the person who needs you, in the birds that sing, in the flowers, in the animals. (*Mother Teresa 1997*)

In 1982, Mellin-Thomas Benedict was diagnosed with inoperable, terminal cancer. While staying in a hospice, he underwent a cardiac arrest, his heart rate not restored for more than half an hour. During efforts to resuscitate him he had a near-death experience. Afterward, he inexplicably began to recover from his cancer. In *The Near-Death Experience: A Reader*, he describes this second stage as a "Void" that was both less than nothing and more than the sum of everything that exists. Like Mother Teresa, he realized that this Void, or silence, is at the heart of all life:

> It took me years after I returned to assimilate any words at all for the Void experience. I can tell you this now: the Void is less than nothing, yet more than everything that is! The Void is absolute zero, chaos forming all possibilities. It is Absolute Consciousness...
> Where is the Void? I know.
> The Void is inside and outside everything. You, right now even while you live, are always inside and outside the Void simultaneously. You don't have to go anywhere or die to get there.

According to Tibetan and Hindu death practices, this stage is an opportunity for us to reunite with the source of all self, life, will, and mind. The Tibetan Buddhist science of death tells us that we have only to surrender to this stage, or put in other terms, choose to identify with it. The essential law of death is elegantly uncomplicated, we become whatever we choose to identify with—or, if we prefer, whatever we surrender to. For a brief while at death, according to the *Tibetan Book of the Dead*, we are given a reprieve from life's turmoil, merging with its source. As it has been written in the *Tibetan Book of the Dead*, "Your other breath stops and you experience reality stark and void like space, your immaculate naked consciousness dawning clear and void without horizon or center." *(Robert Thurman translator 1994)* The text then warns us that if we cannot surrender to this stage we will mistakenly view it as merely a brief lapse into sleep or emptiness. And indeed many near-death survivors describe it in such negative terms. There are occasions when it even elicits fear. Unless we surrender to this stage, the *Tibetan Book of the Dead* explains, we will remain slightly apart from it and therefore envision it only as an impenetrable darkness. Because we are slightly out of sync with this source or ground state, we do not see it as it really is. Only when consciousness perfectly intersects with its source do we really recognize its true nature, which is "empty" not because it is dark but because it is clear—the clear light of the void, as it has been christened in Tibetan Buddhism. Dilgo Khyenste, perhaps the most renowned Buddhist lama of this century, described this source of life as being "like a transparent crystal which takes on the color of whatever cloth it rests on—yellow on a yellow cloth, blue on a blue cloth, and so forth." *(Dilgo Khyentse 1992)* A metaphor from the *Vedas* is frequently employed to describe this consciousness: All life is forged of the same raw gold. Some of us may be forged into jewelry, while others may become statues or coins, but it is all still gold; it just bears a different form. So it is with consciousness. It is the clear "gold" that we are all made from. While alive, we fuse this consciousness with personality, memory, and belief—forming a self. In the second stage of death, this self is again melted into its essential raw gold.

Of Chinese origin, the Tao Te Ching is the most ancient of the earth's scriptures. Listen to the way in which the message of the Tao, which is often translated as the Way-of-all-things or simply, the Way, echoes this stage in the near-death experience:

> There was something formless and perfect
> before the universe was born.
> It is eternally serene and empty,
> and the mother of the universe.
> For lack of a better name,
> I call it Tao. *(Mitchell 1988)*

The Upanishads are the highly refined mystical legacy of India's namelessly ancient saints and seers—many dating to 700 B.C. *Upanishad* is a term composed of the verbal root "to sit" and translates as "sit down close to," which means to sit down at the feet of the guru, who orally imparts sacred wisdom directly into the ear of the disciple. Most of these gurus were forest dwellers, their wisdom frequently cloaked in rural legends and tales. The Upanishads are part folk lore and part deathless wisdom, which repeatedly describes the wonders of a silent "Self" underlying all reality. At the hub of the ever-spinning wheel of Hindu myth, this Self is defined as Brahman, a term which means it is both great and small, as it is both the essential identity of the universe as well as each finite creature dwelling within it. The Self in the Upanishads is viewed from innumerable angles; among them is changelessness in the midst of change and timelessness in the midst of time. In the Prashna Upanishad it is written:

> Those who know the supreme Self as formless,
> without shadow, without impurity,
> know all, gentle friend, and live in all .
> *(Easwaran 1987)*

The Christian mystic Meister Echkardt wrote, "The ground of man is also the ground of God." *(O'Neal 1996)* This second stage of the near-death experience is also revealing our true self—the clear light that is the Self even of God. Saint Teresa of Avila described such an experience as the prayer of quiet. During contemplative prayers her soul would often join with God, whom she described as steady and still, yet an ever-burning consciousness; the same consciousness which burns within all of us, transparently shedding light on our minds and senses. As the Hindu sage Ramana Maharshi said, "Consciousness is always self-consciousness. If you are conscious of anything you are essentially conscious of yourself. Unself-consciousness is a contradiction in terms. It has no existence at all." *(Ramana Maharshi 1988)*

The heart of the ancient Jerusalem temple was an empty room, symbolizing a God beyond all conceivable forms. It was a God whose name could never be uttered, whose image could never be shaped, without committing the sacrilege of deceiving us in regard to God's nature. But as we could also have learned in that temple, God is not merely a stillness, but the invisible power which pours forth the universe. The priests in the Temple of Jerusalem were not comparing God to the empty darkness of the room, but were imparting that God is beyond all such dualities as light and dark, emptiness and fullness.

So in this second phase of the near-death experience, we have already met with the most direct way to the divine—through quieting our inner energies, beginning with the ceaseless waves of thought. By slowing the pace of thought, we learn to see beneath its restless energies. We can, in life, teach ourselves to find this second stage of death within ourselves, so that when it appears after death we will immediately recognize it and easily merge with it. Like all forms of meditation, it is a way, essentially, of working with death while still alive. Quieting our thoughts is merely the beginning, for we must also begin to relax and surrender into this state in order to see it as it really is—clear and powerful. Only then do we realize that it is not merely an emptiness, but contains the energies that our mind states arise directly from. Slowly, then, the mind unmuddies, revealing a perfect clarity—a clarity which is consciousness itself. Following such a path is like watching a photograph slowly developing. Gradually the dark, imageless negative gives way to a vivid brightness and even images, without sacrificing its true nature.

St. John of the Cross called this stage "the dark night of the soul," a kind of inner purgatory the soul is forced to endure as it nears God. It is likened to entering an abyss which stifles all energies and forces we once linked to the divine. Because there are no inner forces or psychological "winds" to propel us across this voidlike passage, we must depend entirely on surrender—on creating an open space within ourselves which the divine can in turn flow into. Only then do we penetrate the darkness and merge with the infinite dawn, the clarity that is the true heart, or nucleus, of consciousness. If we are not capable of fully surrendering to it, then this stage may seem brief, dark, and inconsequential.

Tirelessly, I strove on this meditative path for decades, repeatedly mistaking a vacant, dark mind for this lucid, eternal self. Eventually, I realized that I had to surrender into this state, letting go so profoundly that I identified with it. The night this occurred it was like a light was birthed within me; waters of the self which had appeared morbidly dark were suddenly luminously alive.

I tend to view all spiritual paths as an effort at reconnection of a lesser self with a transcendent identity. It does not require that we annihilate the self we are familiar with, but merely soften its edges so it blends with consciousness itself. So in quieting the mind we are seeking to sharpen consciousness while blunting our self-conceits. But there is no exclusive path to the divine, and any that genuinely serves to "reconnect" us will serve just as well. Relaxing our mind-made self is not the only way to reunite with God. As we examine the next few stages, other ways of uniting with the divine will be discussed. It is crucial to remember that we are each unique and will thrive only if our approach to the divine mirrors our distinct gifts and temperament. If we attempt to embark on a path we are not suited to, we tend to rob our spiritual life of its considerable joy—a joy that may carry us almost effortlessly along if we permit it.

Illustrating this is a famous story that I wish I had taken to heart earlier in my own journey:

> A pilgrim visiting with a famous Indian sage privately asked of him, "Master, how long will it take me to find God if I meditate for two hours a day?"
>
> "It will take twenty years," the master calmly replied.
>
> Discouraged by this answer the pilgrim quickly asked, "What if I meditate for eight hours a day?"
>
> "It will take forty years."
>
> Confused by this answer the pilgrim asked, "But master, why will it take longer?"
>
> "Because you will have taken all the joy out of your spiritual practice."

It is joy that leads us along the path, not harsh discipline. It is not the stars that make the light; the light makes the stars. The universe grew from within itself, beginning with void where consciousness awaited us. We have been told that we need our body in order to exist, but it is our body that needs us. We are not physical beings who have spiritual experiences; we are spiritual beings having a physical experience. And so we begin to see that we must turn all our beliefs around in order to understand the near-death experience.

Stage Three: Entering the Light

Slowly, often imperceptibly to begin with, the emptiness gives way and a light dawns, often with a passageway or tunnel leading to it. In this stage we are drawn toward this light. From far away, a spiritual sunshine falls upon us and we are effortlessly enfolded within it, spiritually gestating in this light throughout the remainder of the near-death event. Like disembodied moths we rise toward light. In Genesis, there is a remarkable echo of this death event as the Bible's first passage rejoices in the transition from darkness to light, from a stage-two state of consciousness to a stage-three. The Bible ushers us into its sacred space: "In the beginning, the earth was without form, and void: and darkness was upon the face of the deep." God's first edict was "Let there be light." The first act God performed was to divide light from darkness, and it is in this stage that most witnesses realize the profound spiritual nature of this post-mortal event. The light itself is a spiritually transcendent signal, an annunciation of a divine reality beyond death. For children of light such as ourselves, finding our way in life through the portals of our eyes and indebted to the light of fire for civilization, such a vision is inexpressibly magnificent—in the afterlife state we are overjoyed to discover an even more glorious light source. Near-death reporters are so enthralled with this light that the term "going toward the light" has become a synonym for the near-death experience. The following near-death narration was found in Melvin Morse's *Closer to the Light:*

> As I reached the source of the light, I could see in. I cannot begin to describe in human terms the feelings I had over what I saw. It was a giant infinite world of calm, and love, and energy, and beauty. It was as though human life was unimportant compared to this. And yet it urged the importance of life at the same time as it solicited death as a means to a different and better life. It was all being, all beauty, all meaning for all existence. It was all the energy of the universe forever in one place. *(Morse 1990)*

In this third stage, for the majority of experiencers, there is a sense of the regeneration of life, the stillness eclipsed by a rapid ascent toward a brilliant light. It is this unmistakable transition from dark to light, a quick reversal of negative and positive imagery, which most people relate most strongly to the near-death event. As the person rises he usually sees a tunnel leading to the light. "It was absolutely black out there and I felt like I was being drawn towards an opening at the end of a tunnel. I knew this because I could see a light at the end." *(Grey 1985)* After this stage, the light, in one form or another, defines the rest of the near-death experience. A remarkable fifteenth-century painting by Hieronymus Bosch titled, "The Ascent into the Empyrean," illustrates this transition. People are weak and perishing in the foreground of the scene, angels hovering protectively over them. In the middle ground of the picture the spirits of the deceased are making the transition, angels guiding them through the tunnel. And in the extreme background are the fortunate souls who have arrived, kneeling in the light to receive its blessing.

The light is usually described as brilliant white, so visually ablaze that most near-death reporters half expect it to be damaging to look upon, but instead they find its radiation pleasurable. Reportedly, the light's whiteness is often tinged with silvers or golds, almost as though delicately filigreed. On rare occasions the light possesses richer, more vibrant tones, the most common of which is blue. Irresistibly, the person is immersed in its living radiance with which the person's inner self seems to be in blissful communion. The light is not just viewed as a source of illumination, it is felt to be living, loving, and supremely wise. Almost invariably the light is perceived as the soul of the universe or its supreme God, its divinity unmistakable. In *Return from Death* appeared this assessment of the light:

> The following series of events appear to happen simultaneously, but in describing them I will have to take them one at a time. The sensation is of a being of some kind, more of a kind of energy, not a character in the sense of another person, but an intelligence with whom it is possible to communicate. Also, in size it just covers the entire vista before you. It totally engulfs everything, you feel enveloped...
>
> But this was the most beautiful feeling I have ever known, it's absolute pure love. Every feeling, every emotion, is just perfect...Everything there is absolutely vivid and clear. What the light communicates to you is a feeling of true, pure love. You experience this for the first time ever. You can't compare it to the love of your wife or the love of your children or even sexual love. Even if all those things were combined, you cannot compare them to the feeling you get from this light. (Grey 1985)

Rushing toward the light, it is not unusual to feel as though one's own energy level is being raised to meet with it, as many powerful vibratory sounds and sensations are often reported. "The closest thing I could probably associate it with is, possibly, the sound of a tornado—a tremendous gushing wind, but almost pulling me." *(Morse and Perry 1990)* Most near-death experiencers miss the relevance of the stage preceding it, but few make that mistake here. The white light is the source of life made visible to itself, which the person tends to recognize wordlessly and merge with. In *Return from Death*, a man who nearly died of a ruptured ulcer while on the operating table relates:

> I found myself in this extremely bright light and felt peace. I feel the light and the peace were one. All I know is that I was there, I'm not afraid of it and that it's something beautiful. I just can't explain it. I don't remember how I got there, just that I was suddenly in the light and it was beautiful. I had no sense of being separate, I was in the light and one with it. *(Grey 1985)*

Often the light is reported at the verge of death, as both a harbinger of spiritual renewal and healing. In *Autobiography of a Yoga*, Paramahansa Yogananda describes being set upon the spiritual path by a near-death experience at the age of eight. As a young boy lying in bed, stricken with cholera, he gazed at a photograph of his father's guru and "saw a blinding light enveloping my body and the entire room. My nausea and other uncontrollable symptoms disappeared; I was well." *(Yogananda 1946)*

During the near-death sequence, people often report that the light takes over, briefly immersing their senses and mind in its radiance. For a brief flash there is only an infinity of light. My own near-death experience revealed to me that all consciousness was really light. Whether it seemed to be light or consciousness depended entirely on whether I was looking *at* it or looking *with* it. Consciousness is what *subjectively* illuminates our life; visible light illuminates *objectively*. Quite simply, consciousness is inner radiance, while visible light is outer radiance. And this stage of the near-death experience is so significant because it is the meeting place of these two radiances. In the second stage, we merged with consciousness. In this third stage consciousness begins to see again, beginning with pure light. Within the cycles of our own consciousness this point is reflected in the movement from a deep sleep to dreams. It is at this threshold between deep sleep and the dream state that consciousness divides itself, invisible light meeting with visible light. Genesis not only poetically reflects the findings of astronomers that the universe arose from a cloud of gas in a black void, but also reflects the way we rise from deep sleep and the way we move toward light at death. Consciousness is the self of light, while light is the self of everything else.

In the death practices of Tibet, this meeting of the two illuminations just after death is referred to as the "meeting of the Mother and Child luminosities." The source, or Mother Luminosity, was briefly revealed in stage two. In this third stage, we see its inner nature made visible to itself as a pure white light. So you may refer to it either as consciousness seeing itself as light or a mother meeting its child. Sogyal Rimpoche, the masterful translator of Tibetan wisdom, likens the second stage to "a sky shrouded in darkness" which, if we recognize it or surrender into it, becomes "like the clarity in an empty sky just before dawn." In this third stage, this radiance is fully manifesting itself so that consciousness begins to "arise in all its splendor, blazing out as energy and light." *(Sogyal Rimpoche 1992)* He likens this transition to being like "riding on the rays of the sun" to bask in the essence of its light—divine love. Near-death experiencers almost invariably use the terms light and love interchangeably. Light is not just consciousness made visible, it is also love made visible. This immersion—not just in light, but unconditional love—is the most powerfully remembered near-death event. For the white light is always with us, even after our return to the body, in the guise of compassion and kindness and love.

According to physics, when all lights in the spectrum coalesce, the sum is white; myriad colors merging into the light that unifies the universe. In such a way, mystics unify their many inner selves to reveal divine love; like the physicists, they are not creating a new reality, they are merely revealing a hidden, unified nature. And it is this sense of deep connectedness that gives rise to love. In *Return from Death* is the testimony of a woman who has just had a fatal heart attack: "I came to the arc of the pure golden love and light. This radiation of love entered me and I was part of it and it was part of me." *(Grey 1985)*

Perhaps no writer has given a better account of the light's divinity than Tracy Cochran. In *Transformations,* she records what transpired within her while she was being strangled by an attacker on a Manhattan street late at night—suddenly light arose from within her to meet with a light far above:

> As I looked up at this light, this presence, it seemed to gaze down upon me, embracing me in loving attention. I felt buoyed up, completely supported by a sea of love and light, yet I was aware that I was part of the sea. I felt searched, and I was certain that what was being searched for was a feeling unknown to me, buried under all the attributes that made me "Tracy." After a time, the light seemed to pour through a particular spot in the center of my chest. I sensed that the deepest, most hidden corner of my nature was being seen at last. This brought with it an extraordinary sensation of being connected to the cosmos, as if I had been delivered from the prison of my isolation and welcomed to take my place in the living world.
>
> I sank to my knees on the sidewalk. This felt right somehow, as if my body was assuming a posture of supplication." *(Cochran and Zaleski 1995)*

Traditionally, the way to the light while on earth is that of meditation. Ancient sources such as the Taoist mystics of China describe a flow of circulating light in the body which makes consciousness possible. Death, according to these texts, is simply this same flow reversed. The light flows out of the body, reunifying with its source as white light. These texts essentially teach ways of mastering this inner flow so that we can enact death while still alive. They are, quite explicitly stated, preparing us for death. Their purpose is to teach us to return to and reunify with the source of light and consciousness. These practices involve ways of getting in touch with this energy or light flow by hearing, feeling, or seeing it within and thereby learning to trace its pathway in the body. Once we involve ourselves in such practices, we supposedly begin reversing the ever-grinding wheel of reality. Instead of our identity being constantly pushed deeper into the body and growing more physical, it is slowly extracted and reunified, growing increasingly more light-like, more spiritual.

Tibetan death literature exhaustively describes the ways in which this light withdraws itself from the physical body at death. It enters and departs, permanently so at death, by way of a channel that flows through the apex of the skull, or what is seen as the soft fontanelle in a newborn. This light is invariably described as "above" us because we reach it by ascending through our own body and leaving through this point. Such treatises on death can be read either as actual, experiential texts, or metaphorically rich journeys into the inner psyche. Both readings can provide us with a "spiritualized" death, as we surrender our inner nature to a unified reality which we may or many not envision as possessing a conscious momentum after death.

In his remarkable autobiography titled, *Kundalini*, Gopi Krishna describes the way in which this same subtle energy ascended along his spine, filling his head with divine light: "Whenever I turned my mental eye upon myself, I invariably perceived a luminous glow within and outside my head in a state of constant vibration, as a jet of an extremely subtle and brilliant substance rising through the spine spread itself out in the cranium, filling and surrounding it with an indescribable radiance." *(Gopi Krishna 1970)*

In his *Confessions*, Saint Augustine describes a similar discovery of this conscious light: "And I entered and beheld with the eye of my soul, above my mind, the Light Unchangeable. He that knows that truth, knows what that light is; and he that knows it, knows eternity." *(Saint Augustine 1953)*

What we have learned thus far is that we can attain reunion by surrendering to the divine, either by stilling our inner energies (finding the divine deep within) or by reversing their flow in the body (rising toward the light of the divine). They are twin paths to the direct recovery of an original self, enactments of a spiritual death while still alive. For untold ages, human beings have followed one of these two paths to mystical reunion with God, and they are reflected perfectly in the second and third stages of the near-death experience. Saint Teresa of Avila referred to this form of mysticism as spiritual marriage, in which the individual soul is a bride and the ineffable God is the groom.

This third stage is ever overflowing itself into the fourth. In the fourth stage, we are about to learn that there is another way of reuniting with this light. This is the way of love. As we learn from the near-death experience, the essence of the light is love itself. Whenever we love, the light is drawn to us and we are drawn to it, setting in motion a gentle pull that will carry us directly into the light at death. By deeply reconnecting with life through serving and loving others, we are also practicing for death just as surely as the rarified practitioner of Taoist or Buddhist meditation. Love, we will learn, is the governing principle of life and the nature of all relationship. And wherever relationship is expressed as a generous and compassionate heart, love again invariably leads to Reunion.

Stage Four: Meeting the Being of Light

When I review the images that congeal into our vision of the near-death experience, I see it as a form of soul flight. Whether or not this journey is psychological or it is actually transcendent travel, the flight itself is unmistakable. Consciousness is launched into its own deepest space, from which it gradually begins to fall away, like a rocket that was not quite able to shed physical gravity. This gravity is our link to the physical body, which has not quite been severed in the near-death experience. The moment finally arrives when the heart starts beating again, oxygen-enriched blood flows, and we are inevitably pulled back toward the physical body. So I tend to view the near-death experience as a psychic trajectory which begins the instant we are thrown out of the physical body in the first stage. From there we plunge directly into the deepest space of all—a sacred emptiness (stage two)—the atmosphere of life itself, or consciousness. As our spiritual arc levels off, we pass into its outer stratosphere of white light (stage three). Now, in the fourth stage, just before our plunge to earth begins to accelerate, we encounter a being of light who provides the vital link between the subtle, luminous divine atmospheres above and the physical ones below. Standing at the threshold of infinite light, this being personifies the divine itself. As we finally rush earthward, we plunge rapidly through celestial paradises, representing the first acts of light's creation. Gradually, then, creation hardens as though in a solar kiln. Just prior to our return to earth, we will be subject to a life review—that is, our life reassembles around us. Only then does the being of light part company with us, after journeying to the brink of physical reality. Finally we find ourselves again in a physical body. But we have been reborn in a sense as a result of our ascent into sacred space. The near-death experience does not just permit us to visit these ethereal spaces, we are transformed, briefly becoming part of them.

In reviewing the near-death stages above, it seems that this fourth stage is perhaps most crucial to those of us who are returning to the physical world. From the light's infinite horizon its own sacred self emerges. In this stage, the light gives birth to itself as the light opens its eyes and sees us, just as we see it—the most primal, sacred relationship is born. We learn here that our first relationship is with the divine in personal form— the myriad relations of the universe arising naturally from it. So we could say that all relationship is an outgrowth of our relation to the divine itself. This link to the divine is what makes love so essential, for without it all relationships are perilous and unfulfilling, only half-realized.

As this stage matures, we "sit down" with this sacred being. If we have no beliefs as to the nature of the divine, this being may remain shapeless. But if we are Jews, it may appear to be Elijah or Moses; if we are Christians, it usually appears as Christ. The *Tibetan Book of the Dead*, meant to be read into the ear of the deceased, reminds us that a Buddha of light can be summoned who will materialize on a ray of light and lead the way to salvation. Whatever form the being takes, it is apparently intended to invoke our trust, to encourage our heartfelt surrender. Without such a surrender, Tibetan sources remind us, the being of light is powerless to help us.

The being of light communicates teachings directly to our minds, we are told, not using words but expressing meaning itself, meaning which words often fail to impart. The realizations that this being most forcefully transmits are love and acceptance:

As the light came towards me, it became a person—yet it wasn't a person. It was a being that radiated. And inside that radiant luminous light which had a silver tint to it— white, with a silver tint to it—(was) what looked like a man...Now, I didn't know exactly who this was, you know, but it was the first person that showed up and I had this feeling that the closer the light got to me, the more awesome and pure this love—this feeling that I would call love... *(Morse and Perry 1992)*

Humanity has always relied upon sages in one form or another for its spiritual sustenance. Mystics, East and West, have depended on spiritual guides from within their own ranks. Such guides use the light of their own inner illumination to show the way. In medieval Europe, Christian monks who had managed to elevate themselves spiritually served as mentors to their brothers and sisters within their orders. Within monasteries, spiritual lineages developed, enabling medieval mysticism to flourish. In the East, the Upanishads were finally recorded as scriptures in the Middle Ages, after centuries of verbal transmission by venerated sages. The Upanishads are the most sacred of India's spiritual teachings. As already mentioned, the term Upanishad itself comes from the root-verb "to sit down," meaning to sit at the feet of a guru who will impart a secret teaching. This is also referred to as *darshan*, which translates as "a thing seen." So the divine teaching is not just heard, it is also seen, the sage himself the embodiment. According to this belief, through this intimacy with a realized soul, we are showered with invisible grace. The being of light is the celestial equivalent of living saints, gurus, and mystic guides—the ultimate spiritual sage, for he embodies the light itself. During the rest of the near-death experience, we "sit with" and receive darshan from this sacred being. We both see and hear wisdom, until the sixth stage, when we are told by this being that we must again take up our body and finish our life's work. Narrators of the near-death event almost invariably describe this being as what affected them most profoundly—

and the grace they were showered with not as invisible, but as a powerful light.

The grace gradually begins to manifest itself as a paradise, the abode of the sacred being. Composed entirely of glorious light, shapes arise, scenes unfold, and the light itself is translated into many ethereal forms. Opulent cities have been reported, but most scenes tend to be more serenely pastoral. Human figures are often seen within the light and it is not unusual to recognize a deceased loved one among them. Panoramas similar to the folk tales of Shambhala or the mythical portrayals of Eden are often recounted, their glory indescribable. The Book of Revelations, in the culminating verses of the Old Testament, describes a city of light called "Holy Jerusalem." Following a glorious description of a city of palaces, robed in jewels and gold, we are told "the city has no need of sun, neither of the moon to shine in it: for the glory of God did lighten it…" In *Return from Death*, we find this testimony of a woman who died while under anesthesia during a dental procedure:

> Then I found myself, I was in a beautiful landscape, the grass is greener than anything seen on earth, it has a special light or glow. The colors are beyond description, the colors here are so drab by comparison. The light is brighter than anything possible to imagine. There are no words to describe it, it's a heavenly light. *(Grey 1985)*

Shortly after my first death experience as an adult, the only friend I confided in who did not believe me to be imagining it or making up tales had recently been involved in a car accident that had almost proved fatal. In confidence, he told me of a light similar to mine, except his was seen "in a heaven." He remembered, "This light energy was everything, God was not the least bit hidden." In this heaven, a being of light informed him that all of reality was made from frequencies of energy, visible only as light. Nor had his experience seemed illusory or dreamlike to him but had been the "most real thing I had ever experienced." As in my friend's case, the near-death survivor views the light as the essence of life itself. According to quantum physics, this may well be true on the physical plane, for the universe is filled with subliminal light energies as well. Our earth reality is only mistakenly perceived as solid, when it is really as immaterial as this heaven. The world discovered after death is a sea of living light that etches itself into panoramas defying description.

Entering this world of the being of light, the perceiver is transformed by it, set on fire with this passion to love and serve unconditionally. Near-death experiencers often describe being changed into light, becoming part of this heaven—they are given the eyes to see light everywhere and a mind which feels the unity of all life. By "sitting near" to the sacred being, they are in turn imbued with spiritual radiance and come to realize that to feel unity is also to feel love; that only by aligning ourselves with unity can we give and receive love, otherwise we are bartering and qualifying love, dancing around it without ever really touching its heart. This being teaches us that to live wisely we must live compassionately. Wisdom cannot be expressed apart from compassion, nor can compassion exist apart from wisdom—they are inseparable. In Buddhism, this is embodied in the image of Avalokiteshvara, the Buddha of Compassion. In Tibetan iconography, he is usually portrayed as a radiant figure with a thousand eyes and arms; the thousand eyes enable him to seek out the suffering of the multitudes and his thousand arms enable him to embrace the afflicted. His power is that he shares the hearts of others, or is co-passionate with them. He rejoices vicariously in their joys and shares all their sorrows. To one who is generously compassionate this is a ceaseless act of reunion.

In this stage, we are shown we have never been separated from our source, we still exist as light even though we are able to act independently. Our independence is always circumscribed, having patterns which fit into life's overall design. And we begin to realize that the meaning of existence is to use our relative independence to express life's unitary nature creatively.

The following account was given by a man who not only was pronounced dead, but whose funeral arrangements were being made. His experience was very complete, as is usually the case with someone who has been "deceased" for a longer period of time. This excerpt is taken from *Life at Death*:

I arrived at a place—it's hard to put into words, but I can only describe it as heaven. It's a place of intense light, a place of intense activity, more like a bustling city than a lonely country scene. While I was there I felt at the center of things. I felt enlightened and cleansed. I felt I could see the point of everything. Everything fitted in, it all made sense, even the dark times. It almost seemed, too, as if the pieces of a jig-saw all fitted together. You know how it is with a tapestry and all the interwoven parts, then when the tapestry's turned over you see how it all fits in place. Suddenly I saw how all my life fitted together to that point. *(Ring 1980)*

The reporter was a devout Christian, who then describes meeting with a Jesus who was very warm and engaging—even humorous. Jesus showed him the palms of his hands and there were nail holes. Jesus remarked, "These are the only manmade things in heaven." He also described the figure he was seeing in this way: "As for Jesus, in that place of light, he was light itself." *(Ring 1980)*

Many have related that even while basking in the loving presence of the being of light, they felt as though their minds were stripped bare by its gaze, revealing every selfish, loveless trait they possessed. We are, it seems, revealed finally to ourselves, our legacy of self-deceits exposed. We see ourselves as we really are, without avoidance or excuses. Yet there is no sense of being judged; only being loved and accepted. The most severe of flaws elicit only compassion. Wordlessly, but in a language of meaning, we are encouraged to learn from our mistakes, but not to expect punishments. The word sin originated from a Greek term which actually translates as "missing the mark." Sin, then, is not that which taints or condemns us, but that which perfects our aim; for as we have spent most of our lives striking near to but missing the mark, we are also learning where the target really is—we are teaching ourselves to find the mark. In *Heading for Omega,* the being of light instructs a dying person on the nature of sin:

> I told him: "I know what's happened, I know that I've died." And he said, "Yes, but you aren't going to be staying here because it is not time for you yet." And I said to him, "This is all so beautiful, this is all so perfect, what about my sins?" And he said to me, "There are no sins. Not in the way you think of them on earth. The only thing that matters here is how you think.
>
> "What's in your heart?" he asked me. And somehow I was immediately able to look into my heart and saw that there was nothing in my heart except love. *(Ring 1984)*

We are given life on earth, it seems, so that we can learn to transcend our flaws and awaken to our self-deceits, for our errors are no more than misdirection and personal illusion, not a matter of evil.

The being of light teaches us that our thoughts, and not our deeds, are what misdirect us in life and plague us after death. Echoed in the near-death experience is a lesson in the power of thought: every thought we have will eventually germinate and so our thoughts must be purified by love, by giving, and by surrender. Almost without fail, the being of light instructs us in the art of thinking. We are told that thought directs energy and is the force responsible for all that we are; our thoughts can either blind us or awaken and illuminate us, they fill our senses so incessantly and uncontrollably that we are caught within their yoke. We are like cattle, driven to our fate by the incessant whip of our thoughts. Our thoughts tighten their grip on our inner self, making it difficult to relax and surrender. As Buddha once reminded an audience, a deed vanishes once it is done, but our thoughts are perpetual—we carry them with us even after our death. So in this fourth stage, we are called upon to learn to direct our thoughts in the service of unified meaning and purpose. In *Embraced by the Light*, the author describes at length the lessons the being of light imparted to her:

> Because our thoughts can affect the eternal energy, they are the source of creation. All creation begins in the mind. It must be thought first. Gifted people use their imagination to create new things; both wonderful and terrible. Some people come to this earth with their powers of imagination already well developed, and I saw that some of them misuse their power here. Some people use negative energy to create harmful things—items or words that can destroy. Others use their imaginations in positive ways, to the betterment of those around them. These people truly create joy and are blessed. There is a literal power in the creations of the mind. Thoughts are deeds. *(Eadie 1992)*

As we stand before this being of light, we are often shown the way in which this feeling of inner unity has become lost. It began with the gift of being able to think independently. This gift enabled us to become creative and powerful. But what we have created has often taken us far away from love. We have personalized our inner lives to such an extent we are usually blinded to all but our own immediate welfare. We have, with our thoughts, confined relationships to those which are most accessible and profitable to us. Because we are out of true relationship with others, we suffer constantly from an emotional insufficiency. From this raw emotional state, fear naturally arises, for what we are unable to relate to invariably seems threatening. It is this raw fear that disconnects us from the grander scheme of life. It is fear that shatters the feeling of unity and love. Our problem, we learn in this stage, is not a matter of sins against life, but disconnection from it. This lesson was brought home to me by a woman of twenty-two with leukemia, whom I cared for many years ago. She was resuscitated several times. The following is from her journal:

> God is only far away from us in our thoughts. We create things for ourselves with our thoughts, rather than for God. That is where we become lost. God has told me that He is everywhere in the world so we can never lose Him. The only private place He has given us is our minds, and it is only there that we create hell. If the world has begun to look like hell it is only because we have put too much of our selfish thought into it.

The near-death experience outlines a cure for our spiritual malaise which is profoundly simple and much easier to enact than we suspect: it is love. A love which redefines life in terms of *ours*, instead of *I* and *mine*. Because the term love has grown so meaninglessly diffuse, we often mistake love for mere sentimentality, lust, desire, or even self-cherishing. Often, we try to love, but find it too imposing a task and abandon our effort. Determining what is or what is not love in any given situation, I often hear, is what is most daunting about it. But the solution is implicitly stated within the near-death experience. The being of light teaches us that what is crucial is not the acts we perform in the name of love, but the intention that grows with them. It is this *intention* to love which is love itself. The being of light requests only that we make the sincere effort to love. Love is effort, attention, sincerity. You give your attention to another, you attend to them. Love is a space from which no creature is excluded.

The Indian sage, Nisargadatta Maharaji, says it this way: "Wisdom tells me I am nothing. Love tells me I am everything. Between the two my life flows."

Jesus asked of us to love our neighbor as we love ourselves. This implies that we must first have love for ourselves and then transmit it to our neighbor in equal measure. Jesus taught that we should reject the notions of self-perfection and absolute spiritual cleanliness—indeed, he reveled in feasts with the most unholy and imperfect, embracing all of life rather than dividing it into the sacred and the profane. He cared only for acceptance of life and unconditional love. Just so, the being of light has shown us that we can examine our flaws, learn from them, and accept them unconditionally. We can then engage this newly nourished inner self and begin to love ourselves. Only from this sense of wholeness that comes from self love can we cultivate love and compassion toward others. This two-fold movement of love, from self to other, may be summarized as follows:

Accept yourself as you truly are, without attempting to conceal traits, without either loathing or aggrandizing yourself.

This self-acceptance allows the elixir of love to bring you into heart-to-heart contact with others. Such a contact is alchemical in that whenever two hearts are joined, they tend to be nourished and healed.

The Dalai Lama of Tibet was once asked how he managed to treat each person he met so compassionately and lovingly, even Chinese politicians who had committed genocide against his people. He replied quite simply, "I view each person I meet as a long-lost relative or friend who I have just been rejoined with." He directs his life toward living in perpetual celebration of this reunion.

Buddha, a self-professed spiritual physician administering to the world's afflictions, taught a form of meditation called loving-kindness. With this meditation, we strive to uproot our self-centeredness by drawing ourselves closer to others on this earth, seeking to forgive and to be forgiven, and in the process we heal our own suffering. I find this a powerful tool to cultivate the love we are told will deliver us into a state of reunion:

All those whom I have injured, intentionally or unintentionally, I ask your forgiveness.

All those who have injured me, intentionally or unintentionally, I forgive you now.

May I be happy. May I be peaceful. May I be free from suffering.

Just as I wish to be happy, so may you be happy.

May you be happy. May you be peaceful. May you be free from suffering.

This meditation is first extended to individuals, probably someone dear whom you already love, such as a mother or child. The wish is then extended in wider and wider circles, becoming more and more inclusive, until it finally encompasses all beings and you attempt to give the love you feel for your mother or child to even an enemy who has harmed or wronged you. In this way we are fully recovered, fully reconnected to life. This sense of relationship will then help to carry us on through our life. Buddha referred to this return to wholeness as "the liberation of the heart—which is love."

All religions intersect at a single point—prayer. The term religion is from the Latin *religio,* which means to link back up. Prayer, then, is the art of relinking our self to our divine source. One cure for our self-serving thought patterns is to pray to be rid of our fear, which the being of light tells us constantly deflects our efforts to truly love. Praying for the grace of love can rid us of our most insidious fears. But praying for the fulfillment of our desires does not; it merely plants them deeper. For a prayer to truly succeed it must be directed away from us and toward others, effectively widening our circle of love. A near-death narrator recounted what he learned about prayer in *Transformed by the Light*:

I asked the light that my cancer would be removed. I prayed actually. And the light said that what we think of as prayers is more like complaining and we are frequently begging not to be punished for something that we are simply going to do again in the future. He asked me to think of my own worst enemy and I did. Then he said to send all my love to my worst enemy. I did and a sudden burst of light went out of me and returned as if it had been reflected back from a mirror...When I finally recovered, the being of light said, now you have prayed for the first time in your life. *(Morse and Perry 1992)*

Prayer contains within it every facet of spirituality; prayer is a healing fount, a form of spiritual discipline, a link with sacred light, and a source of spiritual reunion. When you pray from your heart, you are enacting the lessons of the near-death experience—you are meditating, you are widening the circle of your love, you are surrendering yourself. Prayer is a perfect wheel around which our inner unity turns. Prayer can be a devotional act, addressing our personal image of the being of light, enfolding within it both our yearning for the divine and compassion for others. Prayer is the way we address the being of light when we are again in physical form, requesting guidance. Prayer concentrates our restless minds, restoring our precarious spiritual balance. Concentrating exclusively on a prayer is a form of meditation, while praying in behalf of others teaches us love. The loving-kindness meditation above is a perfect example of this. Prayer escorts us on the spiritual path and it serves as a protecting shield. The art of prayer is inexhaustible.

Prayer is often voiceless, but filled with vivid images. Suitably, the image of light is often used when praying for cures, as illness is imagined to be a darkness which we wash away with a restorative white light. In Tibetan Buddhism, a prayer has arisen named *Tonglen,* which means "giving and receiving." Through an act of selfless generosity, you request that the mental or physical affliction of another be transferred to you. You, in essence, are praying to exchange your inner joy for another's despair. A practice of Tonglen involving successive stages is used to assist the dying. We pray for their recovery, then for their relief from fear and suffering, and finally for a spiritually successful death. At the heart of this practice is imagining their suffering and fear as a dense, grimy black smoke, which we endeavor to draw into ourselves. We attempt to draw all their negative traits into us, replacing them with the white light of whatever positive traits we may possess. Many people might refuse such a practice, worried that this smoke of negativity will infect them. But in reality the practice is designed to be mutually purifying, as the selfless effort and love which generates such a practice transforms and uplifts both individuals.

Like all we meet with in the near-death experience, prayer reflects the art of surrender. Implicitly, beneath all its layers, prayer is an act of love. It is an act that reconnects us with our own divine nature both as everything and nothing. Events in our lives are often uncontrollable; but though we cannot always control what happens to us, we can control the way we respond. All spiritual responses call for a heartfelt surrender. Not that we give in to adversities; we still struggle, but remain mentally relaxed and joined with life. We can then connect with even the most unfortunate events, causing them to resonate spiritually. Misfortune can barricade us inside ourselves if we permit it, but we can also redefine any event by viewing it as a form of relationship—while realizing relationship itself has no bounds. It is this same resonance that transforms the seemingly most unfortunate of events—death itself. As we expand the scope of relationship, we are also reinvisioning the spiritual possibilities offered by both life and death.

Several years ago, a dying young woman illustrated her view of life's possibilities for many of us present. She was in the last stage of a terminal illness. Late in the night she became comatose, but those of us on staff at the hospital were desperately struggling to keep her alive until her father arrived. She had not wanted to be resuscitated, so I sat behind her, holding her in a sitting position; only in that pose could she at least marginally breathe. When her father arrived, he supported her as I had. She was gasping, her heart slowing, when she suddenly opened her eyes and told us that she had been watching us and that we should not grieve. Gesturing to each of us encircling her bed, moving from her mother, to her father, her sister, and finally to me, she expressed her love to each of us. Afterward she again lapsed into coma and soon died. She had briefly rejoined her physical agony so that she could heal us with her love. It was a reverse Tonglen practice, as the dying person was striving to heal our emotional and mental suffering. I have never received a more profound spiritual transmission. This was the epitome of what the death experience teaches as to the necessity of love, even when terrible sacrifices may be required.

I have learned from my work with the terminally ill that all spiritual work is a form of devotion. You devote yourself to your spiritual efforts, surrendering and giving attention to them. When you are fully devoted to a cause you are filled with it, as a worshiper of Jesus is filled with his concept and image, while a person working with the terminally ill is often filled with their demise. There is no way to work with the dying apart from sharing the space of your psyche with them. Eventually their face and yours transpose. It can be harrowing for you to see yourself amid all the ravages of their disease, their face becoming yours as well. But there is also more than ample reward for such efforts. Just as when the being of light requested that the person pray by projecting love to her worst enemy, she was filled with love in return because one is not able to give what one does not possess.

Considerable self-love is necessary to provide care for the dying. For it is all you have to work with as the death process grows more agonizing and raw; it is often difficult not to retreat when confronted with horrendous suffering. A Catholic priest I once befriended gave me a remedy for this. He taught me to pause briefly during such trials, closing my eyes and expressing complete love and acceptance for my inner self. And immediately upon opening my eyes again I invariably found my view of life had been transformed. The more love we have when our eyes are closed and we are alone, the more love we will project when our eyes open again. And if we persist in this unqualified self-acceptance, love will eventually flow from our inner world effortlessly into the outer.

For centuries, humanity has prayed to and worshiped this being of light in the form of a savior or saint. As indicated by the near-death reports, this is not necessarily a mythical relationship; at least at the most critical moment of our lives, at death, we have affirmation that we meet with such a figure and are given guidance and support. Such a transcendent bond seems to exist at the instant we need it most. And by worshiping, yearning for, and dedicating ourselves to this being of light, we draw its divinity to us, its light suffusing our inner lives, and we are granted an invaluable spiritual boon—our inner death is considerably eased. If such a bond is possible at death, I find it very probable it must be during life as well. All worship is an act of surrender, and where there is a loving vehicle for this worship, such as Jesus or Buddha, then it is increasingly personalized and empowered. By praying to such beings we are calling upon their grace. By worshiping their image we give focus to our love, which guides us toward the spiritual "mark." We are effectively liberating ourselves from self-serving desires by directing our hearts toward a symbol for infinity. I have been privileged to meet many genuine lovers of a personal God, and they have often shaken and moved me with their devotion, inspiring me to love in return. Such worship can certainly rejoin us with eternity.

The most celebrated of all Hindu scriptures is the *Bhagavad Gita*, which translates from the Sanskrit as the "Song Celestial." The Gita itself is but a chapter within a tale that sprawls across the mythical history of India and is titled, *Mahabharata*. In this part of the tale, Krishna reveals to his trusted companion Arjuna that he is the divine incarnate. The prince Arjuna's eyes are suddenly opened to Krishna's divine nature while they are poised with vast armies for battle against the usurpers of Arjuna's throne. The fate of their civilization is about to be decided.

Krishna is the prince Arjuna's most trusted councilor and his charioteer for the battle. Krishna seizes the emotionally charged opportunity to impart eternal spiritual teachings, which Arjuna desperately receives, for he and all who are dear to him are in extreme peril. Death's immensity fills the atmosphere between them giving Arjuna the resolve to surrender fully to the teachings, a surrender which such a proud soul as Arjuna may not have been able to manage otherwise. With impending death charging his awareness with extreme lucidity, Arjuna masters the full spectrum of India's forms of yoga. *Yoga* is a Sanskrit term which translates as "to yoke" and refers to spiritual reunion. So Arjuna has learned many ways by which he may attain union, or yoke himself, with the divine. He hears of the yogas of service, action, knowledge, meditation, worship—all of which can be found within the near-death experience. But Krishna closes his immortal speech with advice as to the surest path to salvation: be a lover of God. Many Hindus report meeting Krishna at this stage in their near-death experience, and they often hear the ancient echo of words Krishna once used to awaken Arjuna from his mortal slumber: "If you think of me, I will protect you. You do not need then to bother with any other rules or efforts, for they are meant only to awaken in you this love, which if you direct it to me, then goes beyond all things."

A sacred being appearing in this stage of death embodies every saint and savior on earth, as well as the very self of the divine light. The near-death experience at this stage portrays a mystical convergence of time and timelessness. The line between myth and reality converges at this point, as the being of light is also an allegory for our own spiritual nature. Such a being is not a true story, but is a transcendent one, because he has one foot in time and the other outside it. We learn in this stage the art of love by also learning the craft of self-giving and worship. We all worship at the altar of myth, whether we are aware of it or not. Our psyches are cluttered with cultural icons, legends, and mythical dream-speak. By worshiping a divine image, we surrender our strictly physical view of life, gathering within us a spiritual momentum that will carry us into timeless realms after death. Whether or not this timeless joining is mortally brief or eternal is not within the range of this work to answer, though I suspect there would not be so much pattern to an event that has no purpose.

Some years ago, my mother was diagnosed with a brain tumor after a seizure. The surgeon told us that her illness had gone undetected into an advanced stage. She spent an entire night in surgery, which she was not guaranteed to survive. Afterward her recovery was slow, as she was placed in a drug coma to reduce the swelling in the brain, a ventilator breathing for her. We were told by the physicians that she would be permanently impaired, though we would have to wait to discover its extent. I spent every night I was not working at her bedside.

As I sat with her that first night, I remembered an afternoon I once spent with a priest of the Eastern Orthodox Church. We sat in his study, an archive of ancient Arabic translations of sacred texts, and discussed Christianity, which I confessed to looking upon as a theological maze. He told me that a prayer made famous by an eighteenth-century memoir titled, *The Way of the Pilgrim*, revealed Christianity's hidden core—without which, he explained, the rest of Christianity was a hollow shell. You simply recite the words, "Jesus have mercy upon me." The prayer had arisen in the Egyptian deserts among the first Christian monks, the Desert Fathers, fleeing there in the second century. The prayer, he went on, begins with a prayer of the lips, then gradually grows into a prayer of the mind, and finally matures within you, becoming a prayer of the heart. It is supposed to be recited ceaselessly, much like a mantra, but with the added element of devotional love.

At my mother's bedside, I began reciting that prayer each night until it became a part of me. Soon it recited itself. It became so much a habit that the words flowed almost constantly, taking the place of the usual internal chatter of purposeless thought. When there was a need to think, the prayer stepped aside, only to resume afterward. I shortened the phrase to, "Jesus have mercy," so that I was willing Jesus—or the being of light—to have mercy on whomever my attention happened to fall upon. When I was with my mother, I prayed for her. But often the prayer was directed toward myself or others. I learned more about grief, despair—and love—than I ever had.

I learned another valuable lesson as a result of briefly sharing in the sorrows of the staff. Arriving to visit my mother in intensive care one night, I saw several nurses weeping and embracing in the nurse's station. They seemed to be in collective shock, moving away from each other as though to begin work, only to return again and fall into each other's arms. Later, a nurse apologized to me for her distracted behavior, explaining that one of the staff members had just died. She had been late for work, and assuming she had overslept, they called her home. Her husband told them that when he went to rouse her from her evening nap he had found her dead. She had been relatively young and had been in sound health. A few days later I learned she had suffered a stroke.

It saddened for me the day my mother was finally released from the hospital, her health fully restored. It reminded me of the insubstantial nature of this life. Life is, as many sages say, like a dream, vanishing as inexplicably as it arises. I was reminded that the next breath is never assured and how imperative it is to both prepare yourself for death and set your life in order by sharing love. My mother's recovery was so unusual that when a television station filmed a segment about the surgeon, he asked them to interview my mother as one of his "miracle cures." When asked what she had learned from the ordeal, my mother replied to the interviewer, "to be more loving." Love is what takes care of our life while preparing us for death. Love, more than anything, is that which heals relationships—from the relationships we have with our mother or father, daughter or son, to the relationship we have with death itself.

As I read and reread this fourth stage of the near-death experience, I see the image of Jesus walking the barren desert of Israel, spreading a gospel of unconditional love to a disbelieving world. He seems to me to be the earthly echo of the being of light. They seem to be on parallel paths; one running its course in time, the other running eternally outside time. We learn in this stage that selfless love requires only the sincere intention to love. And though we cannot perfect the world, we can continue to light the fire of intention, bringing it to bear on our lives.

Stage Five: Meeting Your Spirit Guides

The fifth stage tells us this: in any stage along the way we can ask for guidance and it will be given. During any stage of this brief cessation of life, a spirit guide may arise, benevolently offering us support. Such guides can enter any stage in our behalf, and indeed are often reported early in the near-death experience. But I introduce them here, as their role is often to further the teachings of the being of light or to usher in the life review in the sixth stage. Most reporters look upon them as the sacred being's helpers, lesser spirits acting as escorts and protectors in after-death regions.

Judaism began envisioning these protectors as angels, bearing the task of looking after our lives. According to the folklore of Orthodox Jews, we each were followed in life by two angels; one who sat at our right shoulder, recording our righteous acts, and another who sat at our left shoulder, just as faithfully recording our sins. According to this tale, immediately after death a "sunlike being" stepped forward, whose task it was to examine these two records. Many cultures have tales of celestial beings who remain intimately connected with our lives, compiling an account of our deeds. So the efforts of the angels in these mythologies were directed toward carrying us into the sixth stage, where we undergo a life review. Hinduism teaches of two supernatural beings called *shravanas.* And as in the Jewish account, they sit at our shoulders each day, keeping a tally of our deeds and misdeeds. Each night then, when the march of our life's work is briefly interrupted, they report to Chirragupra, the "keeper of the accounts." It is his task then to make the appropriate entries. As you read many such accounts, you get the impression that the angels act as account-keepers, while the being of light then uses this record, not to punish but to teach, "forgiving us for our transgressions."

Such spirit guides, or if you prefer, angels, are often seen as the bearers of light and love, and flourish in every spiritual topography on earth. Winged messengers arise in cultures pre-dating Judaism. The Aztecs viewed these messengers as eagles in light form, acting as escorts to the soul on its afterlife journey. A stone-age tribe of the Philippines had a myth about "Sky People" who were drawn to earth whenever the tribe was in peril. In Tibet, these spirits are portrayed as both peaceful and wrathful deities which can guide or hinder us on our after-life journey, depending on the purity of our minds. Just as ancient cultures held a belief that deceased ancestors or friends serve as spirit guides, paving one's way to heaven, modern near-death accounts echo this sentiment. A woman who nearly died while giving birth relates such a tale in *Transformed by the Light*:

> I began bleeding badly after the birth of my daughter and I was instantly surrounded by medical staff who started working on me. I was in great pain. Then suddenly the pain was gone and I was looking down on them working on me. I heard one doctor say he couldn't find a pulse. Next I was traveling down a tunnel toward a bright light. But I never reached the end of the tunnel. A gentle voice told me I had to go back. Then I met a dear friend, a neighbor from the town that we had left. He also told me to go back. I hit the hospital bed with an electrifying jerk and the pain was back. I was being rushed into an operating theater for surgery to stop the bleeding. It was three weeks later that my husband decided I was well enough to be told that my dear friend in

that other town had died in an accident on the day my daughter was born. (*Morse and Perry 1990*)

Angels traditionally dwell amidst the uncertain terrain between life and death. They are poised there, apparently, because *there* is where most of us are in need of help. Such tales are traceable to our earliest spiritual records. These angels, like the being of light itself, can apparently assume any disguise. They seem to take the shape that our psyche is most at ease with, their reflection arising from the mind's depths. Yet among those professing no belief in the sacred there are reports of "beings of energy," who fulfill all the same roles as the traditional angel. What seems essential to all accounts is this sense of energy or light, which is always mentioned whether or not the figure has a recognizable form. There is often a powerful spiritual current flowing back and forth between the angel and the near-death experiencer. It is apparent that the appearance of the spirit guide arises as much within us as outside us, speaking to us in a visual language we understand and will not fear. From the Venerable Bede, an English church historian, we hear a medieval account which reflects the angels in shining robes seen at the tomb of Jesus:

> He came back to life and sat up—those weeping around the body were very upset and ran away. "I was guided by a handsome man in a shining robe," he said. "When we reached the top of the wall, there was a wide and pleasant meadow, with light flooding in that seemed brighter than daylight or the midday sun. I was very reluctant to leave for I was enraptured by the place's pleasantness and beauty and by the company I saw there. From now on I must live in a completely different way." (*Zaleski 1987*)

Angels exist not only within all stages of death, but also seem to form parentheses around it, as they are frequently seen days and weeks prior to death as well as afterward by grief-stricken relatives and loved ones. "The great advantage of angels," a friend who had been reading up on the subject once told me, "is that they are everywhere." But they almost invariably appear at critical junctions in our lives when we are in despair, gravely ill, or in physical peril, invoking a healing or guiding us to safety. Angel visits have often been reported just prior to death, often foretelling its exact hour. But their usual purpose seems to be to comfort the dying and his or her loved ones before and after death. They serve as messengers from death's nether regions, reassuring us with glimpses of a life continuum unaffected by death. In the remarkable book, *Closer to the Light,* there is a moving story of an eleven-year-old boy dying of lymphoma. Ardent Christian believers, the family gathered in a circle around his bed, praying for him, when the boy raised up and began shouting that he saw God, God's angels, and shepherds. He then told his family that he would soon be safely in this paradise—they should not grieve. His family emerged from their prayer sessions reassured that the boy was safely with God. Also in *Closer to the Light* is the account of a nurse who witnessed the death of a man in his forties:

He was unsedated, fully conscious, and had a low temperature. He was a rather religious person and believed in life after death. We expected him to die, and he probably did, too, as he was asking us to pray for him. In the room where he was lying, there was a staircase leading to the second floor. Suddenly he exclaimed, "See, the angels are coming down the stairs. The glass has fallen and broken." All of us in the room looked toward the staircase where a drinking glass had been placed on one of the steps. As we looked, we saw the glass break into a thousand pieces without any apparent cause. The angels, of course, we did not see. A happy and peaceful expression came over the patient's face, and the next moment he expired. Even after his death, the serene, peaceful expression remained on his face. *(Morse and Perry 1992)*

Many stories relate encounters with angels first in the tunnel, rising to the light. In the Flemish artist Bosch's painting I described earlier, these angels seem to be laboring to arouse each person from a post-mortem daze as they accompany them to the light. Their primary task, according to the vast majority of reports, is to deliver the person to the light. And if the person does not then merge with the light, their spirit guide remains with them. Other near- death experiencers have been visited by angels in the "emptiness" of the second stage of death. Some tell of being aware of an invisible presence joining them in the void which voicelessly conveyed its love and support. In this stage, their minds cannot give form to these beings, nor can they feel them as energy. In later stages, the presence is said to rejoin them, now visible as light and felt as energy. Along the way, angels or spirit guides continue to encourage the person to collect himself, to be more aware. According to the texts on death, as well as near-death experiencers, there is a direct link between our level of attention and the power to see during the death experience. If our attention is weak or distracted, after-death visions reportedly grow dim and murky. This perhaps tells us that we are seeing directly with our awareness in this state, not a pair of eyes, and if we permit our attention to grow distracted, our vision suffers. Concentrating attention is apparently essential.

But there is also an even more essential reason for not permitting attention to wander. Repeatedly, the *Tibetan Book of the Dead* warns the deceased to hold his attention steady so that death's imagery does not begin to confuse him. There are many near-death reports in which the core messages of the experience are lost in a disorienting flood of images. If we are carried away by the mind's random nature after death, it is undoubtedly more difficult to surrender, to remember our spiritual practice, or to pray. We must possess enough steadiness of mind to perform any of these acts. To protect us from ourselves is apparently the angel's primary responsibility, not to protect us from death. An angel's guidance and love prevent fear from arresting us and taking over the near-death state. Once fear overwhelms, a hellish, confusing episode may take place within the overall framework of the death experience. Margot Grey interviewed a man who said, "I was going down, down deep into the earth. There was anger and I felt this horrible fear. Everything was gray and the noise was fearsome..." (*Grey 1985*)

Many who have had a spiritually magnificent near-death experience invariably report a sense of inner peace and feeling deeply loving. The feelings of love and being at peace with oneself seem to be inseparable in the after-death state. But while love is the path to unity, fear is an obstacle to unity. The near-death literature of every age has stressed that the only thing we need protection from after death is our own mind; a mind that is habitually selfish will invoke fear after death, and when fear arises, the mind grows agitated. One simple remedy for this fear and chaos is to learn to cultivate love and not selfishness while alive, so that love and not fear is our habit after death. It seems to be the work of angels, or spirit guides, to draw out our love and waylay our fears so that we may peacefully surrender to the transcendent wonders death holds in store.

Several years ago, I cared for a dying child who had visions of angels. In the beginning it was upsetting to his traditionally educated father. His father was a professor and angels were an affront to his rational mind. Yet when I visited, the father would always update me on the child's most recent visions. What was fascinating about this child's angels was that they constantly changed form. There was no message from these angels; what the child loved was the way they looked. He wanted desperately to share his vision, as he tirelessly drew their images. More enchanting than his drawings, though, was the way in which he breathlessly described his angels. And as his illness progressed, the room grew into a gallery of his angel portraits. As death approached, the child's angels once again changed, this time into remarkable orbs of light. Like suns, or the light at the end of a tunnel. It was not until then that I realized the angels reflected the child's journey, a journey for which he seemed to have fully prepared himself. The child was, in those last weeks, positively luminous. And his father seemed infused with the same joy, the angels having apparently worked their magic on him as well.

In *Beyond the Light*, a woman shares her tale of a first near-death experience as a result of a car accident. During her experience, she met with several spirits who claimed to be helpers and guides assigned to her. They led her to a blazing light. Twelve years later, she went into a hospital to have work done on a hip damaged by arthritis. During the surgery, she apparently suffered a brain injury and for several months afterward she slipped in and out of coma. Throughout this period, she met with the same spirits, who actually began teaching her a spiritual course. These lessons altered her remarkably. She has since been diagnosed as having severe emphysema and adrenal failure. She is virtually unable to move without her wheelchair, yet she glows with life. For she has been given lessons by her spirit guides, or angels, which have told her that her life was chosen by her. She took on these burdens as a way of spiritually advancing herself:

> I chose a big one this lifetime. The spiritual guidance I receive makes living this life possible. I have walked through the dark side and I have no fear of the shadow anymore. *(Atwater 1994)*

Some years ago a friend of mine died in a plane crash. Shortly before his death he began hearing the voice of a spirit guide. And in retrospect it seems that over those months he was being prepared for his own death. At the time it did not seem all that profound to me. His "inner angel" was teaching him to reclaim his own life by ridding himself of false beliefs. "You become what you believe yourself to be," was the spirit's refrain. "If you believe that you are vulnerable and apart from God, then you are. But if you affirm that you are an aspect of God, you rise to that. God draws you to Him." He was told that all that separates us from God is our fear. Almost all our beliefs are fear-based, and once we change these beliefs to reflect a life-affirming vision of God, we are healed of the disease of our fear. And where there is no fear, it becomes apparent that we have never been separate from God.

Many hear spirit voices which teach us to affirm our link with God by changing our belief system. Through reviewing what my friend learned from his inner guide, I was able to realize that being fearless is the same as loving, with a slightly different emphasis: instead of expressing the unity of all life as love, this unity is expressed as a fearless acceptance of life. We must only affirm and believe that we are each part of God, rejecting the negative beliefs that inspire us to wallow in guilt and regrets, thus ignoring life's infinite grandeur. Belief systems that do not accept the divine unity of life teach us self-rejection and inspire us to become false and frustrated in our effort to attain a perfection that does not exist. Then we obsessively hide ourselves from relationship, whereas it is by accepting the boundlessness of our relationships that God is truly recovered. The struggles of life inevitably occur upon a thin line dividing love from fear. And this is exactly where angels tread.

Stage Six: A Life Review

He asked me, "Do you know where you are?" I said, "Yes." And he said, "What is your decision?" When he said that…it was like I knew everything that was stored in my brain. Everything I've ever known from the beginning of my life I immediately knew about. And also what was kind of scary was that I knew that everybody else in the room knew I knew and there was no hiding anything—the good times, the bad times, everything…I had a total complete clear knowledge of everything that had ever happened to me in my life—even little minute things that I had forgotten…just everything, which gave me a better understanding of every-thing at that moment. Everything was so clear.

I realized that there are things that every person is sent to earth to realize and to learn. For instance, to share more love, to be more loving toward one another. To discover that the most important thing is human relationships and love and not materialistic things. And to realize that every single thing you do in your life is recorded and that even though you pass it by, not thinking at the time, it always comes up later. *(Ring 1984)*

Published in *Heading for Omega,* this account reflects the vast majority of recollections of the life review. In Western religions, we generally tend to view the afterlife in terms of punishment and reward; whereas in the East it is viewed in terms of justice. In the East, the person is not cast into heaven or hell, but reaps his karma by taking rebirth. His future life will mirror exactly his transgressions and illusions, the afterlife not an all-or-nothing-at-all proposition, as it is conceived of in the West. But if you reflect on the way in which karma is described, you see that it runs even deeper than exacting justice. According to the law of karma, we are governed by our mind states and wherever we tend to take birth must inevitably reflect these states. Otherwise we would not be drawn to that fate. So karma is not the levying of justice by a "judge," some force outside ourself, but merely states that we have to follow our own minds—our minds are the makers of our reality. It is ignorance, not evil, which leads us astray. If love requires us to surrender these self-limiting mind states, then it must also purify us of our illusions.

The point of convergence between traditions of East and West seems to be love. Love and forbearance also tend to bring about self-liberation. The near-death experience, as well, reflects this possibility, when the person is told there is no punishment but only continuing trials and lessons that seek to reunify our divisive mind states. We hear in the near-death experience echoes of the ancient Gnostic tales of the soul descending into the universe, taking from each planet on its way to earth the qualities it will require in order to succeed at life. Karma, from the near-death perspective, is just the opposite; it is an ascent from life during which we pick up various traits for which we will have to take responsibility. This sixth stage of death reviews our lives, not in a manner that would suggest we will be blamed or praised for what we have done, but rather as a way of reminding us that each breath of life we take carries with it its responsibilities.

In this review, every significant event in one's life unfolds in a single vast panorama. Apparently it is striking to behold, as it is displayed in palpably vivid color, every aspect of it possessing spacial reality. It is literally like reliving our lives, except the entire span of our life melds into one space and time. We can see quite plainly that our life was not merely a sequence of events that ended with death. We find that our life was about something, that it made itself into something. Our life is now transformed into a presence both timeless and spaceless, which includes every deed we have performed, regardless of its relative insignificance. Nothing is forgotten; nothing falls away. At this stage, death reveals to us the masterwork of our life, the hidden product of our labors. As a near-death experiencer once remarked to me, "I was not just looking back upon my whole life, my whole life was there with me."

What near-death experiencers remember most vividly about this review is that they see their life through the eyes of friends, family, lovers. They describe entering the mind of the people who shared their lives and whom their actions most strongly affected, actually experiencing what they felt. The being of light encourages them to reflect on their life's work, not just to survey it. They are encouraged to profit from what they were grateful for in life as well as what they sorrowfully endured. And they find that the tale of their life is quite different from what they expected. In the life review, they harvest a life's work from which they begin a new work. There is no mention of punishment or sin. They are not encouraged to judge themselves, but to listen to and hear the voice of their mistakes, a voice which speaks not of sins committed but of the absence of love that inspired them. From within another's personality they revisit their lives, recalling many forgotten events. With another's pair of eyes and mind as their medium, they are able to reinvision their lives. If they abused or injured another, they stand in that person's place to receive that injury. If they lavished love and care on another, they reap that joy as well. This review is possible, as the being of light has reminded, because of life's essential unity—because one invisible consciousness is the caretaker of every eye in the universe. Like all else in the near-death experience, this stage reveals life's hidden unity by showing us the way our life intersects with those around it. Here we learn to be compassionate, or co-passionate, as we actually share in the passions we aroused in others.

The being of light reviews both our deeds and our motives, yet never judgmentally. Even the most unsavory aspects of our lives are looked upon with loving regard. We are encouraged by the being of light to forgive and in turn accept forgiveness, to let go and go on. We are repeatedly referred to love's touchstones, self-love and self-acceptance. Mirroring our past is meant to awaken in us a sense of responsibility, a desire to work at our inner lives. This life review repeatedly stresses that life is a learning process, that we struggle in order to grow wise. In *Return from Death*, there is this report from a near-death survivor:

My life started to flash before me. I felt embarrassed every time a stupid thing I had done came up. I sensed that the *presence* was saying, "Yes, you did these things, but you were learning at the same time." It was then communicated to me that I should now go back. I didn't want to, but I understood that there was still a lot of work for me to do. *(Grey 1985)*

This life review is meant to inspire us to work to spiritually unfold and give unqualified love. This has been evident to me in every account of the life review I have encountered, and is identical to what Scrooge underwent in Charles Dickens' tale, *A Christmas Carol*. On the night before Christmas, Ebenezer Scrooge is visited by three ghosts who force him to review his life and examine the traits he possessed which caused him to neglect others and to become miserly and neglectful toward himself. Scrooge looked upon money as a barrier between himself and the miserable masses of the world. Yet in setting himself apart from others, he also began to grow barren within, his self-nature drying up. Encountering the three ghosts of Christmas past, present, and future, he begins to see the effect of his deeds. Scrooge visits with others, seeing himself as they see him, weighing the effect of his self-hatred and denial of others. Like a stone thrown into a pond, he is permitted to see the rippling effect that his life has had on others. He learns, as the near-death experiencer learns, that the more selflessly we throw ourselves into the pond of relationship, the richer our lives grow. All survivors of this near-death life review report being encouraged to respond like Scrooge to this vision, returning to life spiritually invigorated and full of selfless generosity.

The vast majority of near-death reporters do claim to respond in this manner, their hearts filled with the same gladness even though they may remain seriously ill. Given this second opportunity at life they strive to feel love and realize life's unity. Often, they describe afterward being inspired to be uncommonly generous with both their time and resources. Such a radical transformation is not born merely of changing the way we behave. We learn that only by completely revising our view of life are we able to transfigure ourselves spiritually. Our self is a centrifugal point which our actions necessarily orbit, never straying far from this image. Our parabola of personal views arises spontaneously from our vision of ourselves. It seems apparent that we must release our hold upon that separate self-image if we ever hope to be completely rid of its afflictions. Minds are fertile soil where beliefs grow, even over the threshold of death. Our task is quite simple really—to let down the barriers, relax, let go, love, enjoy life while giving joy to others. Like Scrooge, most near-death survivors find their view of life irrevocably altered, and though their life's work is still before them, they finally understand what needs to be done. And they often remark that the great relief is not in completing their spiritual task but finding out what that task was in the first place.

In *Beyond the Light*, one woman who passed into a near-death state while under anesthesia echoes the sentiments of Scrooge on Christmas morning:

> My near-death experience had made me quite sensitive to many more things than my mind understands. It also helped me to be less serious about myself. I'm dispensable.

I have discovered that I do not value "things" as I once did. I befriend people in a different way. I respect their choices to be the people they want to be. The same for my own family. I will guide, but not demand. As for the "light"—it was then and remains so, my encounter with the most powerful of all entities. The giver of life on both sides of the curtain. After all, I was given a second chance. I am blessed and cannot ask for more. *(Atwater 1994)*

No matter what is revealed during the life review, there is never a word of blame from the being of light. Perhaps he realizes that any admonishment would simply entrench us deeper in our past habits. It is easy for us to feel inadequate and so give up on such a seemingly immense task as spiritual reformation. We are told to begin our spiritual life, strive to have a generous heart, but most important of all to relax and enjoy. Spiritual work should, after all, be joyously and patiently undertaken. Our goal, I have heard in many near-death tales, is to be on the right path, not to suddenly be at the path's end. In the next stage, we find ourselves again in a physical body, our path beneath our feet, our work resting firmly against our shoulder. The great benefit I see from this brief death and return to life is the resolve to take the next step, shoulder bent to the task at hand, heart and mind secure in what has been discovered.

Stage Seven: Return and Transformation

I went up and up and faded into a deep silver-blue surrounding. Then came something that looked like a big umbrella without a stick. The umbrella seemed to fold around me, and everything became dark. Then, suddenly, I was in a very intense, bright light. I felt warm and loved in a way that I had never felt before. Then I heard a voice from the light: "You've made a mistake. Your life is not yours to take. You must go back." I argued with the voice. "No one cares about me." The answer I got back was shocking. "You're right. No one on this planet cares about you, including your parents. It is your job to care for yourself." *(Morse and Perry 1990)*

This interview appeared in *Closer to the Light*. During the events related, the little girl was just twelve years of age. She was incessantly abused by her parents, a torment she had endured since earliest memory. Her life was so mired in personal atrocities that finally one snowy winter's afternoon she decided to kill herself. She ran her sled down a steep hill directly into a cement bench, her head exposed to the impact. As soon as her head struck, she was ejected from her physical body and found herself floating above the scene. Children from her ghetto gathered, examining her injured body without calling for help, which seemed only to confirm for her the necessity in giving up a pitiless state of existence. But she then heard a voice arising from a brilliant light, which offered her the only advice possible—care for herself. Even more striking was that she emerged from her brush with death with a renewed resolve and sense of purpose, successfully enduring the nightmares of her early life. She felt honest, unconditional love for the first time in her life, after which she was able to start over.

The near-death experience most often serves as a spiritual initiation. The alchemists of medieval Europe viewed spiritual work as an *opus contranaturam,* or a work that goes directly against nature. It is apparent to all of us that physical life has its own logic, which often negates our spiritual efforts. And the near-death experience does confirm that spiritual purposes must often run counter to those in the physical world. Spiritual hope may have seemed unreasonable in the little girl's circumstances, yet without it she would probably have not endured. Her nearness to death gave her a glimpse of what it is like to tap the power of love, revealing a hidden reservoir of life. In the prior stages we were shown the spectrum of unity. In this seventh stage we are returned to a physically fragmented existence. In this stage, as we are returned to our body, we are shown the difference between a spiritual and non-spiritual life, a unitary and a fragmentary way of living—but only after we are given this opportunity to contrast them is wisdom born. So this return is the most crucial of all stages, for we must now unearth the alchemical gold that has been hidden in our own hearts— an excavation which is brought about by surrender and love under adverse circumstances.

The near-death experience can terminate at any point. There is evidence that the experience proceeds only as far as necessary, until the person has been sufficiently transformed. The near-death experience is like the alchemist's fire, to which we are exposed only as long as necessary to burn away the selfish dross of our life, revealing its spiritual essence, after which we are returned, spiritually invigorated, to take up the thread of our life's work. Only then is our transformation put to the test of a physically harsh climate. The tiers of this experience are both psychic and personal, and speak of transcendence and an afterlife. If you look at the evidence merely psychologically, then the goal of the experience seems to be to integrate the many hidden strata of the psyche. But if you examine it spiritually, you see it as a matter of unity and transcendence, of overturning our psyche and pouring it into its deepest source. The distinctions between these approaches can be very subtle. Both are equally valid responses to the near-death experience. And both profoundly overlap. These overlapping transformations I believe to be the core of the near-death experience, not proof of an afterlife or the imagery seen.

Because the seven stages flow seamlessly into one another, when the near-death reporter again falls to earth, these many tiers have integrated themselves at ground zero—the physical experience. We have spiritually unfolded, then enfolded again. This explains the emphasis placed on remaining aware. There is essentially a twofold effort we must make during the near-death experience, one as we rise up the tiers and one as we fall from them. We must surrender as we rise up the scale so we are able to unfold or join with the next tier above. But we must in turn remain aware as we fall or enfold, so that our realization does not disintegrate. Only by remaining fully aware can we bring the integration to the physical plane with us. Exactly like a dream, if there is a lapse in awareness, the dream's message fades away or is garbled. Because you cannot unify all levels without returning to the level that was left out—the physical plane—this last stage is by far the most important. Here our ethereal realizations are grounded and hopefully fulfilled.

A great many mystics seem to recognize this dual nature of spiritual effort, surrender, and awareness. They are interlocking efforts, as increased attentiveness permits us to gather our forces so that we can surrender. But both can meet within the act of surrender as well, for if we surrender, or give our attention to life outside our personal bounds, we have already let go by being aware. To attend to life is to join with it. If you are attentive to others, relationships are almost invariably transformed. Your undivided attention makes others feel secure and cherished, so they tend to let go of their inner resistance. Where there is attention to one another, two selves unify, surrender, love.

The thirty-second attention span supposedly adopted in modern, industrial countries is not born of a defective mind, but of an indifference to others. We have no more than thirty-seconds to spare for anything other than our own mind states. The near-death journey is much like the flight of Icarus in Greek mythology. As soon as we touch the spiritual sun of the white light, our flight is abandoned and we begin plunging toward earth. What saves us from disaster or despair when we find we are once again on the ground is that we have learned to look away from our own psyche. Our inner self has been singed by this flight. And the less there is of this self when we return, the more fully we are able to feel the unity which leads to love and spiritual renewal. Once on earth, though, it is our job not to lose this realization. By being aware of relationship, feeling its unity, and finally feeling and expressing this unity as love, we preserve the near-death state's realizations. Otherwise, the realizations that fell to earth with us will slowly perish.

There are often signs of spiritual regeneration and literal rebirth as a result of the near-death experience. But these transformations can also be wrought by anyone who applies attention and love to their life, especially when they are subjected to extreme or cruel circumstances. I have found that anytime a person applies attention and love to a crisis, a transformation similar to that of the near-death experience occurs. When you can deal with a personal affront or disaster by enlarging your life, by going against your instinct to enclose yourself or strike back, then the same remarkable transformation is set in motion.

Viktor Frankl was a physician imprisoned at Auschwitz death camp when its degeneracy was at its zenith, its rounds of executions ceaseless. Torture, starvation, and deprivation were the way of life recounted by its rare survivors. Yet despite all his personal affronts and terrors, Frankl made a remarkable discovery: where there is spiritual meaning, our inner life can flourish, even in the most brutal of climates, whereas life without spiritual meaning must eventually grow inwardly arid, even pitiable. Near-death experiences remind us that our lives are meaningless because we aridly live as though we were alone in the universe. To remedy this we need only to rejoin the universe, renouncing our view of ourselves as isolated.

Seldom do near-death experiencers report depression, even though they often remain seriously ill, even disabled. As one near-death survivor explained to Raymond Moody, "One thing I learned when I died was that we are all part of one big, living universe. If we think we can hurt another person or another living thing without hurting ourselves, we are sadly mistaken." *(Moody 1975)* Such a person honors life, viewing each act they perform as meaningfully resonant, touching upon the outermost bounds of the universe. Life's meaning is in its resonance, in its echo, in the imprint it leaves on life in general. The near-death experience does not necessarily bring about a magical transformation, but reweds us to our physical universe. The most important part of this transformation is tangible and practical: we begin to think like caretakers of the universe, the earth, our local neighborhood, our neighbors. Near-death reporters tend to flow with life rather than against it, learning to be dependent on the life around them in a way that inspires gratitude and love. Life's brevity, its uncertainties, make it seem all the more precious. Most transformations that occur as a result of the near-death experience are deceptively simple. Only a few entail psychic claims, tantalizing tales, and supernatural abilities. A far greater number of near-death experiencers return simply but supremely human, dedicated to living as sensibly and selflessly as is possible.

If the near-death experiencer comes this far in the experience, a mysterious boundary tends to appear. This boundary is the band that separates the near-death experiencer from "actual death." Once this mysterious boundary is crossed, returning to physical life would be impossible. The near-death experiencer knows without being told that any step taken in this shadow zone is irreversible. Once they begin that journey they have to go on, never looking back. The boundary has been envisioned in myriad ways, such as a dark river, a dense mist, or a fathomless abyss. A means of crossing is always present, such as a bridge or boat. Often, the near-death experiencer is powerfully attracted to what lies beyond the boundary.

This barrier and the means for crossing it fills the earth's mythologies and religions. The legendary River Styx of Greek mythology was just such an image. The boatman Charon ferried the souls of the deceased to the far shore. In Islam we find the Sirat Bridge which spans hell and leads to heaven. The Prophet Mohammed was the first to cross the bridge. The bridge itself acts as a judge toward those who would traverse it. Said to be thinner than a hair and sharper than a sword, the bridge is perilous to cross if the person is burdened with guilt and sin. Only the righteous may cross. Zoroastrian myths tell of a similar bridge, wickedly angled and sharply edged. The person who tries to cross must remain keenly aware and alert. If the mind is distracted by guilt, one will inevitably plunge into the abyss of hell below.

Perhaps one of the most famous near-death stories ever recorded was that of the Lakota Souix shaman, Black Elk. In this story, Black Elk was accidently left in Paris by Buffalo Bill's Wild West Show, which he had joined to learn about white culture. He grew so ill that his coffin was being prepared when we "flew out of his body," catching sight of the infamous boundary between life and death:

> I started to walk and it seemed as though a strong wind
> went under my arms and picked me up. I was in the air,

with outstretched arms, and floating fast. There was a fearful dark river that I had to go over, and I was afraid. It rushed and roared and was full of angry foam. Then I looked down and saw many men and women who were trying to cross this dark and fearful river... *(Black Elk 1932)*

In the *Tibetan Book of the Dead* is described a stage of death which occurs while crossing this final boundary. This stage is referred to as the *bardo* of becoming. *Bardo* is a word that means "in between"—a person is then in between this life and the next. Tibetan accounts repeatedly warn the deceased to remain aware. They tell us that we must not let our minds race out of control, otherwise we will grow distracted and become lost on our journey. And becoming lost, according to the *Tibetan Book of the Dead*, results in being reborn on earth rather than being liberated from the cycle of birth and death.

In the *Tibetan Book of the Dead* as well as the Egyptian and Islamic accounts, what causes us to fail is our own inner weight. It is our own unbalanced conscience that topples us over the edge. The only difference seems to be the way we read the misfortune of becoming lost. Whereas a Western religion tends to read this punitively as a plunge into hell, an Eastern account tends to look upon it as evidence that we have not sufficiently learned life's lessons and so must be reborn and start anew.

Those unfamiliar with or unattracted to mythical images often view this boundary as a band of energy which sets life irrevocably apart from death. There is a sense in almost all accounts, whether or not the boundary is surrounded by a mythological terrain, of this zone being a vibrational shifting point. They realize that once they shift into this vibrational mode there is no going back. Near-death experiencers faced with this dilemma are usually directed to return by either the being of light, or an angel or spirit guide. The reason invariably given is that their life on earth is not yet completed. On occasion, a near-death survivor reports being given a choice of whether or not they will return to life.

In the following account, a woman encounters this boundary and is met by a loved one:

Beyond the mist, I could see people, and their forms were just like they were on earth, and I could see something which one could take to be buildings. The whole thing was permeated with the most gorgeous light—a living, golden yellow, a pale color, not like the harsh gold color we know on earth.

As I approached more closely, I felt certain that I was going through a mist. It was such a wonderful, joyous feeling; there are just no words in human language to describe it. Yet, it wasn't my time to go through the mist, because instantly on the other side appeared my Uncle Carl, who had died many years earlier. He blocked my path, saying, "Go back. Your work on earth has not yet been completed. Go back now." I didn't want to go back, but I had no choice, and immediately I was back in my body. I felt that horrible pain in my chest, and heard my little boy crying, "God, bring my mother back to me." *(Moody 1976)*

The return to life is usually abrupt and visually much less interesting than the vision of the divide between the near-death state and "actual" death. Occasionally, witnesses report a return to their body by way of a tunnel or a reversal of an energy flow. But most people simply find they have been thrust without warning back into their physical body. When leaving my body in my second near-death experience, there was a definite sense of rapidly rising, of expanding; but in returning to the body their was no transition. Within a mere instant I was back inside my body. The quick return was jarring and for a while I found that I could barely see or hear, my legs and arms stiff and unresponsive. It seemed to me that I had been thrown down, but was not quite properly "inside" my body yet so that I could barely function. In my journal I wrote that "my body did not seem to fit properly." I had the distinct sense of having abruptly fallen, my inner self thrown into disarray.

It seems to be quite common for near-death survivors to experience difficulty in mentally adjusting to their situation. Often over days or weeks, there is a sense of being lost in the physical world while their death realizations are slowly grafted to their physical life. Added to this sense of loss may be physical impairments and legacies of pain. And it is not usual for a person to stage minor revolts against the injustice of having to trade such a luminous state for this harsher physical life, often in a body that is physically impaired. Quite the opposite happens in cases in which the person has experienced the life review or has met with angels who counseled about a "life's work"; the transition is usually much easier and the person even feels overjoyed to have another chance to set things right.

It is often reported that friends and family have the most difficulty adjusting to the spiritual rebirth that results from such an experience, for though there is often an inner certainty, there are also just as often outward upheavals upon return from the brink of death. Kenneth Ring has written of a woman in an alcoholic family who underwent a near-death event during surgery. Her deceased father appeared to her, acting as her angel or guide. He led her into the light where she felt illumined and spiritually regenerated. When she returned home after her stay in the hospital, she rejected her family's pattern of addiction. Yet she was unable to sway her husband, as he remained unconvinced of the validity of her near-death experience. They soon divorced. She has since joined Alcoholics Anonymous, acting as a sponsor to new members.

The transformation brought about by my brief death still resounds in my life. Many friends permanently rejected my change, others still look upon it incredulously. Before my death experience, I had several friends who looked up to me as a rough character, always ready for a challenge. Soon after my experience, I no longer desired to prove myself, so that friends who had glorified my life style quickly rejected me. I was set adrift and I had to work to reassemble my life in the image of my after-death experience rather than according to the way I was raised and had come to believe. As a result of my experience, I aroused many internal energies and sensations which had to be surrendered to and slowly integrated into my life. When such after-effects occur, there is a sense of having returned with part of our death still intact—our inner landmarks having moved. Like physical birth, a spiritual birth is often a difficult passage. The psychospiritual rebirth of this seventh stage merely begins with the return to the body, after which you must take responsibility for continuing to give birth to your sacred self. Finally at death, we will again harvest this sacred self, reaping the outcome of this effort.

Upon returning, a rare few find they have become psychic, a situation that often complicates their life. A young girl I knew had a near-death experience which threw her life into utter turmoil. She was a devout Christian who was suddenly appalled by her "psychic" awakening, even viewing it as deviltry. She could not write even a note without "channeling a spirit." Though I most often tend to view these channelings as contact with the unconscious content of our own minds, I also found that this explanation only made matters worse. I was, to her, suggesting that she was deranged. And she preferred the explanation that she was possessed, for she much preferred any spiritual interpretation of what was happening to her over a psychological one. Not until she was able to view this "awakening" as Christian and the spirit as an "angel's" voice was she able to integrate it into her life. After this, the message's language was altered, paraphrasing Christian themes she was familiar with.

Among near-death survivors are the few who make the experience their life's vocation— they become mystics. Many are given afterward to trances, visions, or mystical revelations, which draw them away from the physical world and into a mystical life. Historically, many of the world's greatest mystics received their calling as a result of a near-death encounter. Saint Teresa of Avila and Julian of Norwich were actually in their coffins when they finally returned to life. The more vivid the experience, the stronger the mystical streak seems to be; and the more fully aware we are during the experience, the more potently it seems to affect our spiritual renewal and the more deeply we draw on its power. Such death events seem more likely to give rise to a Buddha or a Saint John of the Cross, or a Ramana Maharshi, an Indian school-boy whose death experience kindled an inner awakening that remained intact his entire life and led him to become one of India's greatest spiritual figures. All cultures have recognized this transformative power of the near-death experience. A shaman's death experience itself is his or her initiation, and symbolic deaths have been used for centuries to install members into secret societies in symbolic imitation of the shaman's rite of passage. The Renaissance masters believed that it was necessary to partake in equal measures of both eternal and temporal aspects of life; the meeting of these two realities giving life greater depth and vitality. Most mystics tend to first walk away from the world, then return, bringing both aspects of human nature finally into conjunction.

Many return from their brief encounter with death with irrepressible "spiritual gifts." Such gifts may involve a calling as a healer, a mystic, or a philanthropist. Many others are given a renewed sense of their life's purpose and strive to be better teachers, laborers, or physicians. The common thread in these accounts is the realization that they have a task in life at which it is imperative they succeed. Life, quite simply, has an urgent purpose. After the light has vanished and the interior silence becomes busy with a life's work, what remains is the sense of unity. In the physical world, we cannot actually see unity or love, we must feel them. This is a much more difficult prospect. When the near-death experiencers were "over there" they did not need to be told that everything was connected, did not have to work at it. Here, on earth, they must pick up the unfinished work of merging temporal and eternal realities. On occasion, this had led to visions of grandeur, but usually results simply in a more well-rounded and dedicated personality.

Regardless of the form their life's work takes, they seem to view this work as an exercise in love, born of the awareness of the unity of all life. The hidden vocation within their work as a factory worker or a teacher is to spiritually reshape their inner self in a loving, generous image. Their real work becomes not the profession they may have rededicated themselves to, but to remake their life into an embodiment of love—one they will be glad to stand before in the life review of the sixth stage.

One gets the impression, listening to the accounts of near-death survivors, that once they fall to earth again the most rewarding phase of their spiritual journey has just begun. During the near-death event, reality was neatly stratified, its many levels apparent. When experiencers return to this life, they find that within themselves all these levels overlay each other. Whereas the flight from the body and its return was clearly marked, putting what they learned into practice is often difficult, even mystifying. In this stage, spiritual practice can become like a labyrinth unless we keep boiling it down to its essence, which is to project love and feel unity.

The megalithic burial stones which are scattered as far East as south India and as far West as northern Ireland were probably erected to conduct funeral rituals. It is probable that these groves of stone were originally mazes, designed to protect a buried king. Eventually it seems, they began to serve as ritual sites where the subjects of the kings learned to follow them into the afterlife. By familiarizing themselves with the labyrinth, they were supposed to have "straightened the way" for themselves when they died. They memorized the quickest route through the labyrinth and relied on it to safely deliver them to the other shore after death. Both life and death can be a maze if we do not straighten the way for ourselves by keeping to the easiest route. The near-death experience, more than any human mysticism, therapy, philosophy, or vision ever conceived, straightens the way for us in both life and death. We are shown the essential path through death.

Part of the secret, I believe, in remaining on the straight way, is to listen to our individuality. If we listen only to the hymn of unity, we cannot straddle both temporal and eternal realities, and we grow out of balance. Listening to our individual nature, we learn to smooth the path for ourselves as well as straighten it, so we neither stress ourselves nor drive ourselves from the spiritual path with the severity of our efforts. In my opinion, it is far more enriching to permit our individuality to flourish rather than to pursue a forced spirituality, such as becoming a monk when we do not possess the temperament for such a vocation. We do not need to radically change our present self to transform the world, we need only to enlarge it. A spiritual stock-broker or physician could perhaps be of more service to the world than a cloistered monk.

An excellent example of the power of unity to transform any trait of skill is the tradition of the Samuri warriors in feudal Japan. Zen realization was grafted to the sturdy tree of Japan's ancient warrior class simply by installing unity at the heart of their creed. The sword, then, usually identified with the annihilation of life, grew to be a symbol of life's sanctity. They learned that only by being aware of the unity of life could they wield such a weapon without imperiling their soul; the samurai's sword signified the spirit that held at bay divisive acts that might prevail over harmony and humanity.

Such a transformation is possible in our society as well, but for it to succeed on a great scale, this realization of unity must occur in every strata of our world, so that people with similar gifts, or shortcomings, can affect each other. In *Transformations,* a story is recounted of an alcoholic named Bill Wilson who was being held in a detoxification ward in New York City in 1934. In the midst of harrowing treatments, he had the following experience, which not only changed his life but has since changed many people's lives. Bill Wilson was later to become a co-founder of Alcoholics Anonymous:

My depression deepened unbearably and finally it seemed to me as though I were at the bottom of the pit...All at once I found myself crying out, "If there is a God, let Him show Himself! I am ready to do anything, anything!"

Suddenly the room lit up with a great white light. I was caught up in an ecstasy which there are no words to describe. It seemed to me, in the mind's eye, that I was on a mountain and that a wind not of air but of spirit was blowing. And then it burst in upon me that I was a free man. Slowly the ecstasy subsided. I lay on the bed, but now for a time I was in another world, a new world of consciousness. All about me and through me there was a wonderful feeling of Presence, and I thought to myself, so this is the God of preachers. *(Cochran and Zaleski 1995)*

Bill Wilson was healed of the torment of his addiction by this vision and spent the remainder of his life sharing his healing with many others similarly afflicted.

This seventh stage is not one of glorious visions, but of real, heartfelt work. It is often more like manual labor than a spiritual flight. We strive, struggle, learn, and grow on earth. Practicing unity and love, being aware and surrendering, are the four corners of the spiritual world. Most of the momentum we meet with in life will directly oppose these forces, attempting to brush them aside. Our spiritual work may be as seemingly ordinary as being a good mother, but there is no doubt that it is as difficult to be a good mother as it is to be a monk or a nun. As long as we continue to carry love and unity with us, our labors will be our greatest source of joy. In *Transformed by the Light* appeared this account of a woman who never actually saw the being of light. Yet the being held her like a child, not only telling her what her work on earth was, but lovingly showing her:

In the midst of all this hospital chaos, I just zoomed out of my body and into a tunnel. I was walking down a tunnel with the most beautiful light at the end that was enveloping and warm. I could feel myself being surrounded by the most loving arms, and my cheek could feel the warmth of a being against whose chest I seemed to be leaning. There were people in the distance and I wanted to greet them. A man's voice, very warm and caring, held me back from going to the people. The voice seemed to be coming from whoever or whatever was holding me in that wonderful loving warmth. The voice said, "Suzanne, turn around." I turned around and saw my children standing in midair. Then the voice said, "Go back and be a good mother." (*Morse and Perry 1992*)

Our individual lives are the refineries of consciousness; our life experiences, the refiner's fire. Our consciousness is the essence of life which can be opened to the universe by the simplest of acts. Spirituality is not necessarily mystical or metaphysical. In Zen lore, sweeping the flagstones is as vital a spiritual currency as worshiping at an altar or silently meditating. Zen practitioners often have *satori,* which are cataclysmic spiritual breakthroughs, but the proper goal of their practice is to unify personal, ordinary acts with life's great wholeness.

I would like to relate a moving account that summarizes the transition into this seventh stage. The near-death reporter is a friend of the author of the book, *Within the Light,* who nearly died in the car accident that killed her husband. She wrote of her remarkable experience in the *Australiands* newsletter:

I returned to my broken body and earth consciousness. I knew where I had been, I knew my husband was dead, and I knew that I would spend the rest of my life pursuing the irresistible force of that transformation. For nine days, I was enveloped in a cocoon of golden light. Unconditional love poured from my heart; I was in a state of grace...

The near death experience continues to live daily in my life. I understand that the uncompleted work for which I have been sent back is to share the unconditional love I was so unconditionally given. I know that God is the totality of life, whether it manifests as Oneness, or trees, grass and people...And that is when the real work began: to address the unfinished business of my life, to learn to become present in my life, to live and die consciously. (Sutherland 1995)

Though we will not all have a near-death experience to awaken our spiritual impulses, we can nonetheless embrace the inevitability of death, not as a morbid preoccupation but as a deepening of life itself. Wisdom-based spiritual traditions tend to view the funeral as the spiritual practitioner's legacy on earth—a litany of his most cherished spirit-invoking images. Just as the theme of the near-death experience is union, religious funeral ceremonies are age-old acts that serve to reconnect us with our spiritual roots. It is the last rite of passage upon earth and a seal upon the spiritual labors of the deceased.

The funeral was not originally intended merely as a ceremony to fill the void left by the deceased, it was intended to serve as a leverage point against death itself, so that the spirit or energy of the departed would be guided into the afterlife. Such works as the *Tibetan Book of the Dead* remind us that the departed spirit is repeatedly drawn to scenes after his death, especially his own funeral, where he is deeply affected by what he overhears or sees. If it is true that in the first stage of death you tend to over-see your own body, it seems also probable that if death continues to unfold and the shadow-zone between life and death is crossed, more may be seen, including the funeral.

The funeral ceremony should reflect as perfectly as is feasible the spiritual aspirations of the deceased. A friend of mine who was an atheist once laughingly asked what sort of image should be displayed at his funeral, to which I answered quite sincerely, "A portrait of Freud." My friend was a philosopher by trade and given to having "peak experiences" or epiphanies. He was also a dedicated follower of Freud; his way of looking into his own psyche was self-analysis. Mysticism was valid for him, but it was temporal and personal, not transcendent. He was as richly a spiritual soul as I have ever known, spiritually generous and rigorously intellectual. He recognized the need for a full-bodied spiritual life, but did not accredit it to a divine power but to the integrative efforts of one's own psyche. As a preventative to psychosis, our minds are always pointing at an inward axis point, pre-verbal—a point of conscious unity prior to diversification of the self. I have no quarrel with his point of view and can neither prove nor disprove it. That it was profoundly spiritual was illuminating to me. To him, all spirituality was merely a matter of symbolic and metaphorical reference to this conscious unity. The difference in our belief systems was that, solely as a result of my near-death experiences, I held to a view of the afterlife and he did not.

If you are a worshiper of Krishna, you should have the suitable trappings at your funeral, rejoicing in the devotion that instilled in you a sense of unity. If you were a Zen Buddhist or Quaker, the affair may be much less layered with symbolism, but there should at least be rituals and images that point toward your spiritual striving. The precincts of the sacred should interpenetrate the event, breathing life into the funeral. If praise or prayer was your passport to the divine, then all the guests at your funeral should gladly sing and pray.

In Buddhism, the funeral and the rites afterward last for forty-nine days, representing the period of time in which the deceased struggles to spiritually awaken the mind, which is prone to dreams and spiritual slumber in this transitional state. Most religions recognize a transition during which the deceased can be assisted on his journey. Postmortem rites and ceremonies should perhaps be performed as a continuation of the funeral itself, perhaps even continuing for a forty-nine day interval. If the funeral is permitted to extend beyond the one day marked for it, then it is also possible that it becomes a channel for grief, permitting loved ones to spiritually engage death rather than merely permit it to engulf their lives.

There is no more auspicious period for spiritual practice than during and after a funeral. At the funeral itself we should perhaps endeavor to take up the practice of the deceased. If the person worshiped Jesus, then we should sing Christian hymns, wholeheartedly performing the worship the departed person cherished most. We must at least assume the deceased is watching us and perform these rituals in their behalf, in order to strengthen their bond with a life-long spiritual practice. The force of our bereavement can be translated into spiritual power if we redirect it through the funeral service. At a Buddhist funeral, though we may not have been Buddhist—perhaps we are Christian—we must strive to remember that Buddha is an archetype of the heart, just as Moses and Christ—a symbol of light itself. After the funeral, perhaps for a period of weeks, perhaps for a forty-nine day interval, you can worship according to your own inclination, praying to Christ to lead the spirit to salvation. I look upon the funeral service as a reflection of the spiritual work that the deceased is undertaking at that moment. After the funeral service, I strive to ally my spiritual path with theirs, in order to create what has been referred to in Buddhism as a "Buddha field," or a space of enlightened activity.

Plato suggested that we spend our life preparing for our death. A spiritual practice I suggest to prepare for dying is to imagine that you have crossed the boundary of the seventh stage into "real death." Imagine as well that you are watching your own funeral. I have found that this practice spiritually directs me to the heart of my life's efforts. Spiritual practice can often grow diffuse and even self-righteous; as a counter weight to this, each time I sit down to meditate, I imagine that I am sitting down next to my own funeral and ask myself what state of mind I want most to possess at this most crucial of moments. This, then, is the state of mind I strive for in my practice. It is quite succinctly an attentive and relaxed love—a surrender. At this moment of all moment's, when we are suspended over death's chasm, it would be sheer folly to manifest any quality that is not the soul of enlightenment itself. Gracefully and attentively surrendering all resistance is all that can serve us once we have stepped across death's threshold, which is exactly the state of mind we want to bring to bear on our spiritual efforts.

If you are devotional in your spiritual practice, I suggest that you imagine that you are with your chosen deity at your funeral. This deity is the personalized image of the being of light, as it appears to an expectant heart. Whether or not the image is of Jesus, Muhammad, Moses, Krishna, the Great Father, or the Divine Mother, make it yours, see the image that is most deeply rooted in your heart. If you are moved, perhaps even to tears, then you have found your heart's archetype for the divine.

Next you might ask of yourself what qualities you want this spiritual figure to see in you when you meet after death. Let this become a moment of self-cultivation. Reflect upon your self-nature, accentuate your desire to love, making the darker aspects of yourself give way to this desire. You may then rouse in yourself the sacred love you wish to radiate both in the relationships of your life and when you meet this figure face to face. In this way you rekindle and purify your spiritual efforts and regain your spiritual bearings.

Finally, and perhaps most importantly, you might imagine observing all those you hold dear. Striving to vividly imagine the scene of your funeral is a wonderful opportunity to reflect on the nature of your relationships. Undoubtedly, you would want family and friends to feel loved, spiritually prosperous, and strong enough to go on without you. You want them to be taken care of materially, but even more so spiritually. What would you wish to have given to others? What wounds would you wish you had healed? What do you wish you had shared? What love do you wish you had expressed, and what sorrows do you feel at deeds left undone? Such questions set against the imagery of your own funeral are emotionally and spiritually charged. The essence of relationship is easily revealed to us when we realize the extreme transitory nature of life.

Death leaves us spiritually naked. Remembering and invoking death by envisioning our own funeral keeps our spiritual practice pure. The funeral is the most deeply felt of all human ceremonies and so can indeed be the most spiritually enriching. It enhances the sanctity of our relationship with the divine and with those with whom we share our lives. Such an image can awaken our sleeping heart, so that our spiritual life is always channeled through our heart instead of our mind.

The Pattern of Sleep and Death

Great waves of sleep pass over the earth each day. A Chinese civilization of more than a billion people climb beneath their blankets each night. As sleep's tide rolls in a clockwise motion, a few hours later millions of Americans on the Western seaboard settle in for a night's sleep. Far behind the tide, in Europe, civilizations are in turn waking up. The unavoidable nature of sleep has prompted many to compare sleep and death. Is not this intermission during a day of life quite similar in nature to the permanent cessation of life at death? Sleep, after all, has all the markings of short-term death. Indeed, Greek mythology portrays these necessities in life as mirror images of each other, portraying Hypnos, or sleep, as the twin brother of Thanatos, or death. In both sleep and death the mind is isolated from the body. Our attention is shifted from the senses to the space the psyche or self occupies in consciousness. Consciousness is both a flow and a constant rise on the horizon of personal life, from which scenes rise before us and recede behind us. The essential path to enlightenment, Buddha taught, was to remain constantly aware of the rise, rather than permitting the mind to wander behind or ahead of itself. Buddha proposed that we stay on that rise, surveying life with care and equanimity. And there is considerable evidence from sleep and dream researchers that if we are able to teach ourselves to remain constantly at the highest point of awareness, then much of sleep and dream can occur consciously.

Every mammal on earth seems to be subject to sleep's dictates. Many grazing animals, such as horses, can actually lock their legs so they can sleep standing. Giraffes, despite their ungainly frames, have to stretch out to sleep. Despite enormous risks—many predators hunt primarily at night—every animal seems to require sleep. Yet there is no known biological purpose for it. The giraffe rises from sleep in an effortful dance that takes up to a minute and makes it extremely vulnerable to the rush of a predator. For ocean-bound, air-breathing mammals the acquisition of sleep requires complex adaptations. If they quit swimming long enough to take a nap they sink beneath the water. When a fur seal sleeps, it swirls about in one place, which is accomplished by moving but one flipper just enough to keep its nose above the water. Even more remarkable is the way in which the fur seal's brain has adapted to the purpose of gaining sleep. Like humans, the fur seal has a brain with two hemispheres. And like the human, each side of the brain controls the opposite side of the body. For example, a human's left brain moves his right arm and leg. To prevent itself from drowning, the fur seal has adapted by letting each half of its brain sleep separately. So when the left flipper is moving, the right side of the brain must remain partially awake, giving the left hemisphere a chance to sleep. After a while the seal switches sides. Mammals such as the Indus dolphin, which inhabit the muddy delta where the Indus River pours into the Arabian sea, never stop swimming. Its life is a life of perpetual motion. Yet electrical recordings of the brain of the Indus dolphin show that it still sleeps as much as seven hours a day; but sleep occurs in very short bursts, lasting as little as four seconds and reaching a maximum duration of sixty seconds. There is evidence, despite the lack of discernable brain waves, that even insects require sleep. Each night, the sea slug retreats to a particular spot, assumes a particular body posture, and remains immobile until the dawn breaks. To even the untrained eye, the sea slug looks to be asleep. The Mediterranean flour moth settles in each night as well, turning slowly in upon itself as sleep progresses, until finally it holds a pose with its sensitive antennae folded beneath its wings.

The neurological maneuvering often required and the sheer enormity of each creature's sleep phase—from twenty to seventy percent of their life—tells us that sleep is vitally ingrained in our nature. It is, according to all evidence, part and parcel of our conscious self. Without sleep there would be no consciousness, it seems quite apparent. The patterns of sleep do not merely go on within consciousness, otherwise many creatures would simply omit sleep as too cumbersome. No, it seems apparent from the evidence that sleep is the nature of consciousness itself. Without sleep, the physical being quickly dies. Yet most of us fail to notice that sleep is not only necessary to us, it is deeply vital. Actually, it would not be too much to say that nothing else in our lives is as imperative to us. We can control our sex drive, can give up our survival instinct, many have even fasted until death. Yet we have no control over sleep; even when a brief nap may imperil our life, we can still only stave off sleep for a short while. Sleep is one of two things in our lives to which everyone succumbs—the other is death.

During the summer I turned twenty years of age, I underwent three near-death experiences in rapid succession. Because near-death studies had not yet been published, I had no way of interpreting what had happened. But I was sure that I had undergone an inner cataclysm touching upon death. There were even physical symptoms of my brush with death afterwards: a constant burning in my nervous system as though it had been singed by some unspeakable power. It was as though my life was poised over an interior fault line that perpetually shifted beneath me—I was filled with unfamiliar energies and images. I had been taken from my narrow view of reality and initiated into a grandeur I never suspected to have existed. I had visited with the underworlds and overworlds of consciousness, returning with many of its psychic energies still with me. In sleep, I began to revisit these realities, having what are commonly referred to as out-of-body journeys. Within these psychically empowered out-of-body worlds light rose to the surface, so that scenes were self-illumined. I felt both cursed and blessed. I both dreaded and looked forward to a night's sleep.

It was difficult to ascertain the way in which these tumultuous, creative energies and fiery inner mind states related to the rest of my life. I kept a journal in an effort to track and understand my experiences. It grew to hundreds of pages rather quickly in those early years. Typically, the out-of-body state arose when I was on the verge of sleep. On sleep's brink, there is always a sense of letting go of the body as you relax into yourself—drawn deeper and deeper in the eddies of the psyche. But when I would relax my hold on the physical body in preparation for sleep, I would rise out of it, looking down upon it from above as in the first stage of the death experience; my psyche seemingly shifted away from physical reality. If I remained aware, not letting my attention wander, I found myself in a state that gave all appearances of being an alternative reality; if my attention did begin to wander I would begin to dream. These dreams were exactly like those we normally have at night, except that they occurred outside physical reality. Often, I would have a half-and-half experience in which I seemed to be both dreaming and sensing physical reality from outside it. There would then be a mixture of dream images and actual objects, so that I might notice the chair in my room, but there might also be a cat curled in it that I did not own. When I was not careful to remain at the peak of awareness, my vision would tend to blur as well, creating gaps which dreamlike images would begin to fill in. It was apparent to me that this out-of-body state was both the place where we dream and where the first stage of death occurs. Dreaming, I found, was the threshold between life and death. The word threshold translates as "the place were things are thrashed or beaten apart." This seemed to me to be an accurate label. Like death, moving into the dream state seemed to break down my normal waking consciousness into its psychic parts. And like death, when I returned to the waking state, these parts were assembled.

Reviewing the journal, I began noticing a consistent similarity between death and the ordinary affair of going to sleep each night. Not only was I describing the first out-of-body stage of the death experience, but I also noticed many flashing lights and lapses into a state of emptiness just prior to sleep. There were even occasions in which I would rapidly glimpse scenes of light, similar to those seen in the fourth stage of death. Inexplicably, I had grown more internally aware, which permitted me to watch myself going to sleep. And I realized that these transitions into sleep were undoubtedly not unique, that they must represent a predictable unfolding of consciousness in sleep. Like death, sleep had an orderly progression of stages. And these stages were remarkably similar to the pattern of death itself.

What finally convinced me that death and sleep shared their nature was a forceful current that began arising during my out-of-body experiences. It always began with a darkness, as though being left alone in a void. In this state, I felt a pull—as though I was being irresistibly drawn away. I immediately recognized this force as the tunnel-effect of the near-death experience that draws you toward the light. Anyone who has ever undergone a near-death experience could never mistake this powerful current. A woman described this force to Kenneth Ring in this way:

> The first thing I remember was a tremendous rushing sound, a tremendous…It's hard to find the right words to describe. The closest thing that I could possibly associate it with is, possibly the sound of a tornado—a tremendous gushing wind, but almost pulling me. And I was being pulled into a narrow point from a wide area. *(Ring 1982)*

Gradually, this pull or undercurrent of death began to threaten me whenever I was in the out-of-body state. I was not so much afraid of death as I was not yet prepared for it. There were still mysteries about death in need of addressing. Eventually I learned to master death's current. It was only necessary to still the mind or to let go of thought. I had begun practicing a form of meditation in which I had learned to briefly still the flow of thought. When this flow was halted, I would immediately terminate the out-of-body experience, plunging into a state of deep sleep. Years later, in the *Tibetan Book of the Dead*, I learned that this out-of-body state was made of thought. This text actually describes this letting go of the mind as leading to liberation at death; apparently as we let go of the mind, it in turn has to release its grasp upon us, so that its mind-made delusions no longer mislead us after death. This pull or force, I realized, was the momentum that leads you through the seven stages of death.

I finally happened upon a text on yoga which clarified the matter. The book was on the subject of Hindu tantra, a path of yoga filled with symbolism and allusions that relies on controlling psychic energy. According to this text, its title unfortunately forgotten, death and sleep followed the exact same route. To master sleep was also to master death. And within the book was described a yoga of sleep, ways by which we can learn to watch our own sleep, remaining constantly aware of our inner states. It was considered a short-cut to spiritual realization because all you had to do was teach yourself to remain aware in sleep. Because these are the same states, though considerably magnified, which rise to meet us at death, the practitioner becomes fully familiar with them and so is prepared for death.

The author gave a highly concentrated formula for the unity of sleep and death—it was the sacred symbol AUM, first conceived of in the Upanishads and figuring prominently in the Tibetan texts as well. The most venerable symbol for spirituality in the East, Aum literally spells out the way infinity has translated itself into the field of time. The Aum sound, pronounced "Om," is a thunderous overture from which every other vibration arises. The Amen sound is a remarkable mirror of this resonating note. The three principle letters in Sanskrit each represent a primary stage of being. "A" stands for waking consciousness, while "U" symbolizes dream states and "M" deep, dreamless sleep. In Sanskrit, there is also an after-sound, the rumbling *echo* of the "M" which is represented by a dot over the word. This fourth state, the transcendental self beyond the mind, denotes the unity of all three letters.

According to Eastern thought, these three notes of *AUM* are not just the substrata of consciousness but also make up the hierarchy of all creation. These are the three sheaths or coats that each of us wears over life's unity. First, corresponding to *A,* is a gross physical sheath or coat, which we refer to as the waking state. The second sheath, *U,* is the mind sheath, full of the images of energy and light, and corresponds to the dream state. When you pass into the second sheath you see a white light; then you begin to see the manifestations of this energy, or you begin to dream. The third sheath, *M,* is the clear, empty ground of consciousness, which corresponds to deep sleep, beyond dream. These three sheaths comprise one indivisible selfhood, the same unity denoted by the dot above the three letters *AUM.* We seldom notice their unity because we are fixed within this material reality where states of mind arise sequentially. On earth we experience one thing at a time, so that sleep, dreams, and the waking state each seem to be distinct; whereas in the near-death experience, reality is timeless. This is exemplified in the life review when the events of one's life are not seen as sequential, isolated moments, but are experienced simultaneously and seem to coexist with the experiencer outside of time.

When I was finally able to compare this yoga manual to death texts from Tibet, I found that in the near-death experience the same three sheaths are stripped away, revealing our hidden nature. When we are initially thrown out of our physical body at death, the letter *A,* or the physical sheath is removed and we join with a dream state represented by the letter *U.* For a brief while our physical body remains visible to us. Then we shift quickly away, proceeding directly to the source of deep sleep, the *M* of *AUM.* Here we have no visible sheath, we only have consciousness. From this source state we descend again to the letter *U*. Because our link with physical reality has been severed, we see a light-filled, psychospiritual reality instead of our own physical form. We learn the lesson of the dot floating over the three letters, as a being of light teaches us the necessity of recognizing unity and living for love. Finally, we return again to the letter *A*, our death experience complete, having been a circular flow through all the possible levels of existence.

The final pieces fell into place years later when I was on staff in a sleep laboratory. In such a setting, we search for evidence of sleep disorders, recording brain waves, respiratory patterns, muscle tone, heart rate, and oxygenation. The machine was a relic from the hospital's dim past, its recordings ink scratches on reams of graph paper. Once a study was in progress, my role was a matter of patiently noting whenever there was a break in the respiratory rhythm or a change in the sleep state. I grew familiar with the circadian rhythms and brain waves that are the signatures of the sleep phases. These phases are set, unfolding in the same way each night. There are five phases within sleep, and like divers we submerge ourselves in them successively, returning to physical awareness in the same way. They vary in duration, but the pattern itself is never altered. We always enter and leave these stages in this same order.

I began to see sleep as a perfect reflection of death, as one by one we take off the coats we wear over consciousness. When the physical coat is removed, our familiar self is replaced with a dream self. Instead of having waking experiences, we have dreams. This state is usually referred to as REM, because in this state there is "rapid eye movement." The rest of the body is virtually paralyzed, but the eyes twitch back and forth as though scanning across an inner scene. The other four sleep phases are non-REM, or non-dream sleep—we see images throughout these phases but only in REM do these images become storylike plays during which we take on the disguise of another self, more mythical and intuitive, often acting out improbable events and gaining insights we do not normally possess. Over all, during the first hours of sleep, there is a pattern of shifting in and out of various phases, but toward dawn our dream state dominates. So the further we move away from the waking mind, the more fully we assume this dream self.

In the first phase of non-REM sleep, the brain waves are similar to the waking state, with rapid, jagged patterns. This is a corridor between drowsiness and actual sleep; awareness fluctuates in this state, moored neither to a waking nor a sleep reality. In phases two and three, the brain waves slow considerably, becoming larger as we sink more deeply into dreamless sleep; here we begin to merge with the clear light of emptiness, but we are most fully merged with it in phase four when we are resting on the bottom of the ocean of sleep. We stay awhile in phase four and then begin to resurface, the phases reversing themselves until we again arrive at phase one, or the surface of sleep. But this time, phase one is replaced with REM sleep—so where an identity close to the waking self formerly was, there is now a dream self. For the remainder of the night, we repeatedly plunge from this platform of REM sleep into the phases of deeper, dreamless sleep, and back again. Finally, at the end of a night's sleep, we break through our dream self and find ourselves awake—we slip back into the garment of our familiar waking self. The dream state is typically the last phase of sleep we encounter each night.

This is strikingly similar to what near-death experiencers report. As we first break away from the physical body within the sleep cycle, we find ourself in a half-waking and half-dream state; in the first stage of the near-death experience we find ourself separated from life but still attached to physical reality, often viewing our own body and surroundings from a distance. Then we merge with the "emptiness" or "void" in the second stage of death, which is analogous to deep, dreamless sleep, most fully attained in the depth of phase four sleep. During sleep, we assume the dream body, mercurial and insightful, which repeatedly leaves its vivid dream reality to enter the deeper waters of dream sleep; this is reflected in the near-death experience as the psychic energy body that shifts from emptiness and absorption in pure light to watching scenes unfold in the plays of the life review and encounters with angel guides. And from both sleep and death, we are returned rather abruptly to a waking self that is perceived as a much narrower, physically defined state of consciousness.

Interestingly, we can be awakened from any phase of sleep; but if we are permitted to awaken naturally, we do so directly from REM sleep, and awaken more refreshed, with much stronger recollection of dreams and more opportunity for inner growth. We can also return from the near-death experience directly from any stage, but there often seems to be more closure and continuity if stage six, the life review, has first been encountered. This seems to me, in both sleep and death, to be the natural stepping off point, where the dream self reintegrates with its physical counterpart.

One important difference, I think, is that when we are merely asleep, we are still grounded in physical reality. Most dreams reflect physical events, and physical sensations during sleep are often incorporated into our dreams. For example, a blanket rubbing against a shoulder may manifest in our dream as brushing against a horse's mane, especially if we have seen or been reminded of a horse prior to sleep, whereas in the near-death experience, the physical link is completely severed.

There is considerable research to support that the more aware we are of our dreams, the more they tend to be meaningful and integrative. Meaningful dreams are described as more rich visually because we are more lucid, or aware, than we usually are when we dream. During such dreams, the dreamer can even gain control of his dream, shaping its image and events. The fact that dreams are intensified and flourish when more consciousness is given to them may well verify that the dream state is not a less conscious, secondary state, but is as equally valid as waking reality. Otherwise, growing more conscious during a dream should cause us to "wake up," rather than empower the dream. In *Where People Fly and Water Runs Uphill*, Jeremy Taylor writes: "In the lucid dream state, the 'awakened' dreamer can generate amazing insights and release extraordinary creative energies. Old habits can be transformed, energies can be mobilized and directed, problems can be solved and transcended, denials and repressions can be raised to consciousness and withdrawn, and confusing feelings, emotions, and intuitions can be clarified and harmonized." *(Taylor 1992)*

This describes a restored unity and meaning that reflects, to a slightly lesser extent, what the near-death experience evokes. Each night, according to psychologists like Carl Jung, "If one watches the meaningful design (of our dreams) over a period of time, one can observe a hidden regulating or directing tendency at work, creating a slow, imperceptible process of psychic growth." *(Jung 1964)* Our dream self, according to Jung, is trying to bring our waking self back into harmony with a deeper, more comprehensive identity in a process he calls "individuation." Individuation, then, is the psychological equivalent of the spiritual reunion elucidated by the near-death experience. Many accounts of lucid dreams read very much like the recollections of "heaven" by near-death experiencers—the colors vivid, light arising directly from perceived objects. The English writer Hugh Colloway recorded his experiences of lucid dreaming at the turn of the twentieth century. He was sixteen years old when he had his first lucid dream, which pictured a scene near his home, where tall trees ran near to a sea bay. Later his dreams turned into out-of-body journeys, which he wrote about extensively under the name of Oliver Fox. He realized that the quality of the dream was profoundly enhanced as soon as he became aware he was dreaming:

Instantly, the vividness of life increased hundredfold. Never had sea and sky and trees shone with such glamorous beauty; even the commonplace houses seemed alive and mystically beautiful. Never had I felt so absolutely well, so clear-brained, so impressibly free! The sensation was exquisite beyond words but only lasted a few minutes and I awoke. *(Fox 1962)*

During lucid dreams the white light often appears. This light has often been responsible for remarkable physical healings and inner transformations. In *Our Dreaming Mind,* the author, Robert Van de Castle, points out, "When light appears in a lucid dream the dreamer typically reports some form of transcendent experience." In the same book, he describes the way in which a former student reportedly was healed from a debilitating lung infection during a dream:

> I saw a sudden spot of light and watched as it came closer to me, growing in intensity and size. It grew until it covered me, felt hot in the center of my chest, made my eyes burn with its brightness and gave me a feeling that I was being healed. *(Van de Castle 1994)*

In her book on dream work, Janice Baylis describes a healing dream of her own in which the light arose directly from the dream's imagery to heal her of a pain in her right eye. One afternoon when she did not report to work because of her pain, she was taking a nap and the following dream occurred:

> I am looking at a bubble of water on our patio. A fish is swimming in it…The bubble changes to a spotted light with a dark center. It begins to move toward me. I am very glad that I am going to be immersed in that light. As the light reaches me I feel a tingling, electrified sensation, strongly centered in my right eye. *(Bayliss 1977)*

Studies have shown that we may be more mentally active while asleep than awake. Similarly, witnesses to mystical or near-death experiences assert that consciousness is quickened and expanded when it is separated from the body. They testify that apart from the body, the mind is far more powerful, the senses considerably more far-reaching. According to sleep researchers the mind is very active except during deep sleep. We have conversations with ourselves, remember things, even remind ourselves of things in the middle stages of non-REM sleep, while we are shuttling back and forth between deep sleep and the intuitive personality of our dream self. Our minds creatively churn during sleep, we just tend to forget our dreams or we are not intuitive enough when we wake up to interpret them. It takes considerable creative power to assemble a dream, a power we all seem to possess. Yet we usually lack the means to tap into this inner resource. Oral evidence strongly suggests that dreams can indeed solve troubling riddles, even scientific ones. One such story is the famous discovery of the benzine ring by the German chemist Frederich von Stradniz. The benzine ring's molecular structure was one of the most baffling riddles of chemistry in the nineteenth century. In 1890, Von Stradiniz affirmed rumors to the Congress of Science that he had made the discovery of the ring-shaped molecule during a dream. In this dream, he saw atoms whirling before him, meeting and forming long chains, which is the usual way organic molecules organize. But then the many long chains began writhing like snakes, and from among their mass one flew forward, grabbing its own tail in a ring-like form, which began to spin before his mind's eye. He awoke, having discovered the elusive design of the benzine molecule.

Similar stories abound in history, and if you remember that less then one percent of our dreams are remembered upon awakening, consider the possibilities lost. Robert Louis Stevenson claims that almost the entire plot of *The Strange Case of Dr. Jekyll and Mr. Hyde* was given to him in a single dream. The dualism of these two characters reflects remarkably on the twin selves of our waking and dream state. It was as though his own psyche was composing a self-portrait, reminding us that the two halves of self must remain in balance if we are to function sanely and healthily. Unity of self is the message of the tale.

Sleep is, according to research as well as tales such as these, a volatile space in which great inner upheavals occur and tremendous insights often arise. Our vision of sleep as a stilted or impaired state of consciousness often prevents us from benefiting from the powerful energies within its domain. The desire to remember dreams and to be more aware is usually sufficient to begin to bring many of these insights into the light of day.

Deeply affected by a trauma, coma, anaesthetics, terror, heart attack, depression, or even meditation, the mind may simply let go of its familiar state of consciousness. Consciousness does not shatter, but falls away from physical reality in stages, like a rocket jettisoning its fuel tanks. Reportedly, there is an acceleration of consciousness, not a slowing down. And there is an unmistakable sense of an inner unfolding. Unlike sleep, the near-death experience sheds physical reality altogether and so instead of seeming to be inside it, it seems to be outside and around it. The nightly rumbling of myth, divine energy, and reunion brightly arises and overtakes physical reality in the near-death experience. Whereas sleep often seems to sift through the depths of mind, the near-death experience inverts mind, revealing the consciousness and energy beyond mind. The patterns of consciousness are with us always, rhythmically *arising* as sleep, dreams, and the waking state. When there is any sufficient jarring of our present pattern, it is only natural that these deeper states begin to arise, regardless of the cause. In sleep, we preview these deeper states, but dreams are usually more a matter of integration, which is more personal, rather than reunion, which is transpersonal in nature, transcending the individual psyche. Yet because they are of the same nature, sleep and death will always overlap, revealing hidden wellsprings of meaning, love, and unity.

Whether or not these realities are perishable or eternal, they are undeniably real and without them we are lost. The angst-ridden world is withering at its roots because we deny that these roots are transcendentally deep. We do not have to overcome physical reality to grow sane again; we have only to reunite it with psychospiritual realities that fill our own inner spaces. The magic of the near-death experience is not irrational; it is trans-rational in that it brings our rational and irrational halves into accord. This results in inner unity or self-love, which then gives us a vantage point from which to project love to others.

Deep sleep is our embryonic nature, whereas dreams are our mythical, energetic nature, and the waking state is our working, earthy nature. By engaging the work before us on this earth we can unify our inner nature. This work is not a matter of change but a matter of self-acceptance. We can know reality by dividing it into parts, but we can know it better by putting them together. To keep our spiritual work honest, I think we must also keep it simple.

I would like to relate to you the first lucid dream ever reported in the Christian tradition, which shows us the way in which sleep and death intersect. In a letter written by Saint Augustine in 415, he spoke of a Roman physician who had grown depressed over the matter of life and death. In the first of two dreams, which the physician described as more real than anything he had ever experienced, he was met by a beautiful youth. The youth took him to a city where he saw a heavenly afterlife. The next night he dreamed of the same youth again. And the dream was once again so vivid he asked the youth whether it was taking place in his waking life or in his sleep. To which the youth replied, "In sleep." When the physician asked where his body was, the youth replied, "In bed." And then the youth explained:

> Asleep and lying in bed, these eyes of your body are now unemployed and doing nothing, and yet you have eyes with which to behold me, and enjoy this vision; so, after death, while your bodily eyes shall be wholly inactive, there shall be in you a life by which you will still live, and a faculty of perception by which you still perceive. Beware, therefore, after this of harboring doubts as to whether the life of man shall continue after death.

The Death Experience and Shabd Yoga

Physical death occurs when the body's integrity is breached; from within by disease or from without by mishap. Physical life requires a precarious balance. If our body's systems are sufficiently harmed, they veer too far away from their balance point to maintain life—we die. As the Greek Orthodox funeral service reminds us, in words that are dreadfully explicit, "the earth that fed you, now shall eat you." With this chant resonating over fresh-turned earth, the mourners register their acceptance of this cycle of give-and-take by consuming mixed fruits, nuts, and seeds. At death the earth is harvesting us, as we harvest wheat after its cycle of birth, growth, and death. We are reunited with mother earth, a figure in mythology portrayed as both sublimely loving and indifferently harsh, according to which season of our life we are in. In India's pantheon of deities, this mother-image has many forms, including the goddess of death, Kali, who wears a belt of human skulls. She has also been referred to as the thief of breath, for it was the cessation of breath which, in ancient beliefs, seemingly brought life to a close.

But a death cosmology such as has arisen in Tibet, India, China, as well as the many tribal cultures scattered over the earth, would say that the departure of the physical breath is only death's first stride. Death's second step is the departure of the inner, psychic breath, which has nourished our consciousness and been responsible for the three-tiered cycle of sleep, dream, and wakefulness—together the cartography of consciousness. As this inner death unfolds, the three stages of consciousness again merge with their source just as the physical body does at death. And like the physical body, the psychic elemental aspects are again re-animated from a brief relaxation into the depth of the universe.

In a material culture, death is judged as the moment of cessation of the physical or *outer* breath. In a spiritual culture, death is reckoned as the moment of departure of the *inner* breath, which rapidly follows on the heels of the first cessation.

In this chapter I would like to discuss this "inner death." Our psychological death, or if you permit, psychospiritual death, unfolds across the first three of the stages we explored in the near-death experience. We described a pull or force that arises in the second stage of death. Most often, it is envisioned as a tunnel or shapeless conduit of force which draws a person out of a black void and toward a light. The *Tibetan Book of the Dead* speaks of this as a moment of bliss, as all the energies (or "psychic winds" as it is usually interpreted) that constitute our psyche are released from the body and rush toward their source. According to Tibetan thought, the pull or power that drives us on is not arising from the light, rather it arises from within us. We flow out of the psychic matrix we have lived within over our life span and rapidly vacate our physical body. Our psyche is drawn to its source but is itself responsible for the "winds" or forces that drive it there. The rush of force in this tunnel is most often compared to a "wind" in the near-death reports, as it is repeatedly likened to a hurricane, tornado, cyclone, or storm.

As this account in *Life After Life* describes it:

> The first thing that happened—it was real quick—was that I went through the dark, black vacuum at super speed. You could compare it to a tunnel, I guess. I felt like I was riding on a roller-coaster train at an amusement park, going through this tunnel at tremendous speed. (*Moody 1975*)

Often, the tunnel phase is also filled with unusual energy sensations or vibrations, which seems to be responsible for the tremendous speed. The force of this energy is usually experienced as bliss or joy. In this next account, which is fairly typical, the reporter describes unearthly "music." The music has been interpreted as the sound that the energies make, while the light is viewed as the source of the energy:

> I knew that I was either dead or going to die. But then something happened. It was so immense, so powerful, that I gave up on my life to see what it was. I wanted to venture into this experience, which started as a drifting into what only could be described as a long tunnel of light. But it wasn't just light, it was a protective passage of energy with intense brightness at the end, which I wanted to look into, to touch. There were no sounds of any earthly thing. Only the sounds of serenity, of a strange music like I had never heard. A soothing symphony of indescribable beauty blended with the light I was approaching. *(Grey 1985)*

According to Tibetan sources, as long as these energies are in the body, they circulate rhythmically as an inner breath. But when these energies are released from this pattern they rush, like winds, toward higher energy plateaus. They "rise," or move toward subtler energy expressions, as this flow from gross to subtle is the path of least resistance for these psychic energies. From the *Tibetan Book of the Dead*:

> At this time when the mind and body are parting ways, pure reality manifests in subtle, dazzling visions (and sounds), vividly experienced…. Thus, whatever sounds, lights, and rays come at you, they cannot hurt you… If you do not know the key of this instruction, you will not recognize the sounds, lights, and rays, and you will wander in the life cycle. *(Robert Thurman 1994)*

Yet it was not in the *Tibetan Book of the Dead* that I found a death practice that illuminated the nature of what occurs immediately after death; it was in the practice of *shabd yoga,* one of the oldest of all yogic practices. The meditation of shabd yoga translates roughly as "union with celestial flow of sound." Shabd is an outgrowth of tantric yoga, or energy yoga. Early tantra masters realized that the essential spirit animating the mind and body was not held within, like a genie within a lamp, but flows in and out, rhythmically filling the body with its force. According to tantra, the life energy, or inner breath, enters the body in the region of the middle of the head and from there flows down the front of the spine before rising again along the back of the spine. Its ebb and flow nourishes the subtle nature of consciousness, which is spread throughout every nerve and fiber in the body. It is the descending force that striates consciousness into the three levels of sleep, dream, and wakefulness. When consciousness is in a state analogous to deep sleep, it is static but filled with potential; when consciousness is then raised, it is likened to the dream state in which it expresses itself dynamically, fulfilling its potential; in the waking state consciousness grows dense, energy itself compacted into mere physical form. This energy, according to tantra, is tangible as it rises and falls through the planes of the body: it is *felt* as subtle vibration; it is *seen* as subtle light; and it is *heard* as subtle sound.

Shabd yoga is grounded in this philosophy of tantra but emphasizes the aspect of the inner energy as sound. The most famous proponent of this yoga was the medieval mystic Kabir, born to a poor Muslim weaver in Benares, the holiest of India's cities. The term *shabd* has also been translated as the primal "Word" or "Name of God" and teaches the art of self-willed death for the purpose of bringing one nearer to God. In such a practice, one plunges into deep meditation, resting attention solely on the inner sound, the vibratory hum of the subtle energy within. As Kabir wrote of this magical sound:

> *Catch your shabd,*
> *Your origin and essence;*
> *the ocean will then*

merge with the drop,
The part will contain the whole,
like the seed that holds within it
a mighty tree.

Such is the nature of shabd,
like a magnet it pulls the soul.

This primal sound has been referred to in innumerable sources apart from this yoga. In the *Book of the Hopi*, published in 1963, there are passages that make it plain that the peoples of the southwest have long been familiar with the inner sound:

> The living body of man and the living body of the earth were constructed in the same way. Through each ran an axis being a backbone, which controlled the equilibrium of his movements and functions. Along the axis were several vibratory centers which echoed the primordial sound of life throughout the universe or sounded a warning if anything went wrong.

Pythagoras believed that we are filled with the Music of the Spheres, which sustains us from birth. The Essene Gospel recently unearthed and translated from the Arabic, states: "in the beginning was God, and the sound was with God, and the sound was God." In the Upanishads, the holy sound or name is repeatedly pointed outward, using the gesture of many names, but the most celebrated of them is Aum (or Om). Mohammed heard the divine melody in the cave of Gira-Hira, where a host of angels channeled the Koran to him. And the mystics of Islam, the Sufis, refer to this sound as *saute surmad,* "the tone that fills the universe." Buddhist sutras speak of this sound as "the intrinsic sound of your mind essence." Shamans since a primordial age have transformed this sound in their trances into the vision of an animal, which they then ride into post-mortal regions. This inner sound expresses itself in innumerable ways, encompassing many sounds, music, and tones; but in its most concentrated form, it makes a sound similar in nature to the resonating last note of the chanted Aum or Om—a sound which is like the roar of thunder. Om is usually used to refer to the blending overture of all sounds—an infinitely resonating hum. The terms *Om* and *shabd* are often used interchangeably. When AUM is written out in three letters it symbolizes the unity of sleep, dream, and waking consciousness; when it is symbolized as Om it refers to the underlying energy of these three states expressed as sound. The famous Indian Swami Nityananda, who roamed homelessly, rarely speaking, delivered his only teachings while in a trance. Among these was this one on the nature of the Om sound.

> *Om vibrates like a storm in the sky.*
> *having neither beginning or end,*
> *it is the stage manager of the divine drama.*
> *The sound, though truly one and undivided,*
> *can manifest as many—*
> *the roar of the sea,*
> *notes on the flute, violin, harmonium,*
> *beating of drums or bells,*
> *even the hum of bees.*
> *These are ten sounds*
> *of the one subtle sound invisible.*

Intrigued by this energy as sound, I began to meditate in the tradition of shabd yoga. Over several years, both alone and with my wife, I experimented with this form of meditation. What I discovered was that shabd meditation affords a glimpse of the near-death experience from a slightly different angle. Shabd meditation involves lengthy sessions, as it requires both endurance and concentrative skill to complete the practice. An entire evening spent in meditation is not unusual. Plugging the ears in order to block outer sound is the first step in the practice, followed by adopting a pose that can be comfortably held for an extended period. Then it is a matter of holding attention in the middle of the brain—at the target-area where thought and the senses of sight and sound seem to converge. It is this mid-point in the head which seems to be the home of the self and it is here we must steady our attention while listening to the subtle sounds that arise behind plugged ears.

At first a distant ringing or hum is heard. The ringing is a nerve sound, the hum can be identified as the pulsation of the carotid artery. But if attention remains fixed on this point, eventually subtler sounds begin to arise. As your concentration settles, these subtle sounds grow forceful, drowning out the sound of nerves and artery. This is what Kabir referred to in his poems as the "unstruck sound," which to begin with usually bears a distinct resemblance to the chirp of crickets or sparrows. The first time I heard this chirping, it was as though a flock of sparrows had descended around me and I opened my eyes, breaking my concentration. Gradually the sounds grow more complex and ethereal—rain, surf, wind, and musical sounds like bells, flutes, violins, sitars, and occasionally the blowing of a conch shell. The more fixedly attention is held at the mid-point of the head, the more these sounds manifest.

But two other sensations arise as well. First, lights of various colors may begin to undulate in this space, seemingly full of breath and life as they perpetually sway and flow across the mind's eye. There is a sense of a void being brought to life, as the thoughts of the mind are replaced with energies, both audible and visual. Then, perhaps even more remarkable, a numbness begins consuming the body. This is similar to the numbness of a limb gone to "sleep," but is far more profound and rises in distinct stages. This is first sensed in the feet and lower legs, preceded by intense pain, as though all the life is rising to the surface. It requires considerable fortitude to bear the pain. But when the legs and feet are "asleep," it is as though they have vanished, as though you do not exist below the knees. As you remain concentrated on the mid-point of the brain, this numbness slowly rises to the upper legs, then groin, the arms, abdomen, and chest. Finally it progresses to a point where there is no feeling of having a self below the level of the mid-brain. All that seems to exist is this point of consciousness in the brain, suspended within a void—yet there is no sense of having a brain or head. All the energy of consciousness once circulating throughout the body is now condensed at this point within the head. At this juncture a distant roar is heard, like thunder approaching from below, and a rising force sweeps upward through the body at great speed. As it rushes through the head it gathers that focused consciousness and carries it away through the top of the head. And here, in this state of disembodied consciousness, I have encountered both the light of the near-death experience and its manifestation, a being of light.

Indeed, this practice of shabd meditation very clearly initiates the same events that occur in the near-death experience. What obviously distinguishes the two is the actual physical death that sets the near-death experience into motion. In the first stage of the near-death experience we are thrown from the body, and often see our own body before us, whereas in shabd meditation, we have not suffered this physical death and so we bypass this first stage. It is the psychic or inner death which begins stage two that is enacted through the practice of shabd. In this second stage of death, according to tantra, we are drawn back into the body, all our energies slowly gathering at one location (the mid-point of the head, in shabd), then carried out of the body by a powerful ascending force. Kalu Rimpoche, in his masterful translation of several works on Tibetan death practices has written: "The different vital factors that sustain life deteriorate and disappear at the end of a lifetime. During the bardo (at the moment of death), the various winds (or energies) that animate the body are destroyed. Another wind then manifests, called the wind of karma and becoming. It is usually diffused throughout the whole body." He goes on to explain that consciousness temporarily dissolves into an emptiness because there is no energy to animate it. Then the wind (or energy) of karma arises and sweeps us from the physical body. He even describes "a sound that arises from this wind that is a terrifying sound, louder than a thousand thunderclaps…this deafening sound is the sound of emptiness." *(Kalu Rimpoche 1997)* It seems apparent that the pull or force that carries us through the stages of the near-death experience is this karmic wind and is the same force created within shabd meditation which draws our energies to one point to mimic the death process.

The model of shabd yoga has provided for me the hidden pattern of what happens in the near-death experience between the second and third stage, as well as offering evidence that the near-death event was an actual, psychophysical and spiritual event. It supported my research on sleep and dreams. In texts on yoga, I had read that sleep and dream states were the result of a natural cyclic energy migration in the body, which drew consciousness into its own depths. In dreams, subtler energies dominate over physical, and in deep sleep energies are quieted and unified. And it is surrender to these energies rather than resistance at death which liberates us from our own self-deluding mind states. By lovingly surrendering to these energies as they are drawn toward their source at death, we can be liberated from the repetitious cycles of sleep and death.

> *I have found something,*
> *something rare have I found;*
> *Its value none can access.*
>
> *I dwell in it, it dwells in me,*
> *we are one, like water*
> *mixed with water.*
> *He who knows it,*
> *will never die;*
>
> *He who knows it not,*
> *dies again and again.*

—Kabir

Beyond the Seven Stages: Reunion and Love

> *For one human being to love another;*
> *That is perhaps the most difficult of all tasks,*
> *The ultimate, the last test and proof,*
> *The work for which all other work is but preparation.*

> —*Ranier Maria Rilke*

What I believe to be the focus of the near-death experience is the indivisibility of all life. We learn that a river of divine consciousness flows through all of life, without which there would be only darkness. During this brief interim between life and death, we learn that we carry within ourselves a great spiritual possibility and a great obligation—we have been told in the voices of countless near-death survivors to infuse every act in our life with love. We are asked by the being of light to love, but we must first ask of ourselves, "What is this love exactly?"

I once had a friend from India who introduced me to a traditional Indian game called Snakes and Ladders. Popular with children, it is played with a pair of dice and a gameboard. With each throw of the dice, the player is entitled to move his marker across a board of one-hundred squares, each square embellished with a statement such as Glad Company, Seat of the Blessed, Virtuous Disposition, or negatives like Avarice, Greed, Shame, and Evil Disposition. It is a contest of luck in which the gameboard is a stylized representation of spiritual development and the object of the game is to find passage to liberation from selfish illusions, and reunion with the divine source of life. There is considerable danger as well as providence in this geometry of squares. The danger is painted as snakes with yawning, insatiable jaws. And the providence is depicted as ladders lending a short-cut over life's many dangers. A player can climb many squares by landing at the bottom of a ladder and ascending rungs. But a player landing in the mouth of a snake must slide down its back to a much lower square.

For many years, I carried within my mind's eye an image of living upon that gameboard. I was struggling in my life to rise from the bottom of this gameboard on planet earth to the celestial freedom at square one-hundred. Anytime I spiritually prospered, achieving a rarified state of consciousness in my meditation, I presumed that I had stepped upon a ladder. And whenever I was distracted or held onto a dense, earthy state of consciousness, I assumed that I had slid down a snake. I was constantly playing this game with myself. I was seeking to rise to the highest square on the board and remain there.

One night while working in the intensive care nursery, a death occurred that changed my view of life forever. A baby girl with many visible birth defects was brought in from another local hospital. Because the child was born out of wedlock and was bi-racial, no father or grandparents chose to visit. The baby had so many genetic errors written into her life that a rapid death soon became inevitable. Permission was received finally to remove the child from all life-support, but as the mother remained at the other hospital, there was no parent to hold the baby while she died. So I volunteered. Sitting in a rocking chair I was given the baby to hold. I began rocking her, but this seemed to aggravate her pain. Finally I just sat still, awkwardly clutching the infant. I then remembered what a physician had once told me about a baby in the womb. Apparently our ears are our most vital sense in the womb, so that we enter life by way of our hearing. We hear the lit world outside before we ever perceive it. And, I suddenly remembered, the world within is paced by, is filled with the incessant rhythm of a mother's heart. The drum of the mother's heart is as magical as any shaman's drum (which is probably what makes the shaman's rituals so effective). It alludes to the transitional state between life and death. So I held the baby closer, pressing her tiny ear to my heart. The baby grew calm and when she finally stopped breathing my heart momentarily stopped, for we had grown psychically attached, of this I had no doubt. We had met, heart to heart. We were, briefly, spiritual lovers.

After going home that night I pondered her death. I had found love with that baby, but what was it, in what way could I define it? And suddenly I knew. We had completely filled each other's consciousness, my attention had been completely on the infant and hers in turn had been completely absorbed in me. The way to love was not through sentimentality or concepts about love, but was consciousness itself when it was permitted to flow naturally. When I give you my full, undivided attention, I am giving you love. I realized finally that our responsibility in life is not to transcend everything by rising to the hundredth square on the gameboard, but to realize our unity with the board itself. The goal was not the last square on the board, but to engage fully the entire board and every square upon it—to engage all of life. That was the lesson of love that a tiny baby had taught me.

Love is a sacred marriage, a reunion of our own consciousness with that of the world. According to the near-death story, love is always with us, a fount that never runs dry and is available to us every moment of every day. Love is the first energy, nourishing all that exists. At birth, we each begin a journey toward reclaiming this love. If love is this force that animates all life, then aspiring to embrace it should not be as much like pushing a burden or traversing an uncharted wilderness as simply looking to ourselves and closing a circle we have left open. We are, when we love, completing the circle of ourselves—we are finding reunion. We often do not find love in our lives because we have forgotten what it looks like. We tend to imagine spiritual love in the guise of a saint kneeling at an altar, in extreme penance, or in self-annihilating sacrifices. Yet if love is our very essence, then why would it involve a penance or pain?

If we try to love perfectly, it becomes like a veneer over our minds which merely coats our relentless self-invovlement. Genuine love is honest, slightly ragged from bearing the brunt of life's many turmoils. It never perfects itself nor rises like a star, but is more like the rock-solid earth we stand upon, the foundation of life itself. Life is not healed when we try to overwhelm it with our efforts but when we firmly stand upon it. The firm stance is born of seeing deeply. When we look deeply enough into anything, we see unity. Everything is linked to everything else, all life is like the quilts my grandmother used to sew from rags, the hundreds and hundreds of ragged, imperfect pieces making perfection. Apart from everything, there is no perfection. As the modern Buddha, Thich Nhat Hanh has put it:

> When we stand facing the ocean, we may feel small and insignificant compared to the ocean. When we contemplate a sky filled with stars, we may have the impression that we are nothing at all. But the thought that the cosmos are big and we are small is just an idea. It belongs to our mind and not to reality. When we look deeply at a flower we can see the whole cosmos contained in it. One petal is the whole of the flower and the whole of the universe. In one speck of dust are many Buddha lands. When we practice that kind of meditation, our ideas about small, large, one, and many, will vanish. *(Thich Nhat Hanh 1996)*

Love is born of the congealing moments of a day, in the thoughtfulness we put into tiny acts, the gentle simplicity of our intentions. Love is seldom about dying for our child or our mother, but is always about listening to them, even when they are angry or trying our patience. Love is addressing the needs of others with the totality of ourselves and the fullness of our attention. Every breath, every thought, each glance, each word, can be infused with love. As we learned in the near-death experience, love thrives in relationship. But not just in the big moments of relationship; it also grows in the tiny moments flowing into each other. All loving acts, great and small, are composed of tiny moments of patience and kindness. The small things in life are what make up the great things. And where the small things intersect with the great things, we cannot help but realize and express love. Love arises naturally when we realize everything is part of the vast unity of God. As Mother Teresa, a great exponent of selfless love in our time, has expressed it:

> We (the Missionaries of Charity) are called to be con-templatives in the heart of the world by:
> Seeking the face of God in everything, everyone, every-where, all the time, and his hand in every happening. (*Mother Teresa 1997*)

When I was a small child, there were several children throw-ing stones at a baby sparrow on a clothes line. I struggled with them to stop, but finally in exasperation I threw a stone at the line, hoping to frighten the sparrow away. My stone instead struck the sparrow and killed it, and the children laughed at me and danced gleefully around the sparrow crumpled upon the grass. I sat most of the afternoon with the tiny corpse in my shirt and wept, both humiliated and grief-stricken. Many years later, I had several conversations with a priest who asked me about the things I regretted most about my life—I mentioned the sparrow. He took me to a place in the forest and we sat on the earth, in intimate company with the trees. We were in a shaded grove of vividly growing, struggling life forms. Later I would realize he had invited me there to give illustration to what he was about to say. Finally he reached out a finger and gently prodded me over the heart, saying, "Whenever you respect the unity of life, love is born. Your love of life can heal anything for you. And where there is love death cannot enter." I realized then, I still loved the sparrows.

Atwater, P. M. H. *Beyond the Light: What Isn't Being Said about the Near-Death Experience.* New York: Birch Lane Press, 1994.

Saint Augustine. *Confessions.* Catholic University Press, 1953.

Bailey, Lee W., and Yates, Jenny. *The Near-Death Experience: A Reader.* New York & London: Rutledge, 1996.

Bayliss, Janice. *Sleep on it! The Practical Side of Dreaming.* California: De Vorss & Company, 1977.

Berman, Phillip. *The Journey Home.* New York: Simon & Schuster, 1996.

Black Elk. *Black Elk Speaks: As Told to John Neihardt.* New York: Washington Square Press, 1972.

Chopra, Deepak. *The Path of Love.* New York: Harmony Books, 1997.

Cochran, Traci, and Zaleski, Jeff. *Transformations.* New York: Bell Tower, 1995.

Darling, David. *Soul Searching.* New York & Toronto: Villard Books, 1995.

Eadie, Betty. *Embraced by the Light.* California: Gold Leaf Press, 1992.

Easwaran, Eknath. *The Upanishads.* California: Niligiri Press, 1987.

Easwaran, Eknath. *Dialogue with Death.* California: Niligiri Press, 1981.

Fox, Oliver. *Astral Projection.* New Hyde Park, New York: University Books, 1962.

Frankl, Viktor. *Man's Search for Meaning.* New York: Hoder & Stroughton, 1987.

Gackenbach, Jane, from *Deamtime and Dreamwork,* edited S. Krippner. Los Angeles: Jeremy Tarcher, 1990.

Grey, Margot. *Return from Death: An Exploration of the Near-Death Experience.* London: Arkana, 1985.

Hahn, Thich Nhat. *Cultivating the Mind of Love.* Berkeley, California: Parallax Press, 1996.

Happold, F. C. *Mysticism: A Study and an Anthology.* London: Pelican Books, 1963.

Kalweit, Hogler. *Dreamtime and Inner Space.* Boston: Shambhala Publications, 1988.

Jung, Carl G. *Man and His Symbols.* New York: Dell Publishing, 1964.

Kabir. *A Touch of Grace: Songs of Kabir.* Translated by Linda Hess and Shukdev Singh. Boston & London: Shambhala Press, 1994.

Kellehear, Allan. *Experiences Near Death: Beyond Medicine and Religion.* Oxford & New York: Oxford University Press, 1996.

Kelsey, Mark. *The Dark Speech of the Spirit.* New York: Doubleday, 1968.

Kubler-Ross, Elizabeth. *The Wheel of Life: A Memoir of Living and Dying.* New York: Scribner, 1997.

Krishna, Gopi. *Kundalini: The Evolutionary Energy in Man.* Berkley: Shambhala, 1970.

Khyenste, Dilgo. *The Heart Treasure of the Enlighened Ones.* Boston: Shambhala , 1992.

Levine, Stephen. *A Year to Live.* New York: Bell Tower, 1997.

Nisargadatta Maharaj. *The Experience of Nothingness.* San Diego: Blue Dove Press, 1996.

Mitchell, Stephen. *Tao Te Ching.* New York: Harper & Row, 1988.

Mitchell, Stephen. *The Selected Poetry of Ranier Maria Rilke.* New York: Random House, 1982.

Moody, Raymond. *Life after Life: The Investigation of a Phemonenon—Survival of Bodily Death.* Covington, Georgia: Mockingbird Books, 1975.

Morse, Melvin, and Perry, Paul. *Closer to the Light: Learning from Children's Near-Death Experiences.* New York: Villard, 1990.

Morse, Melvin, and Perry, Paul. *Transformed by the Light: The Powerful Effect of the Near-Death Experience on People's Lives.* New York: Villard, 1992.

O'Neal, David. *Meister Eckhart, from Whom God Hid Nothing.* Boston & London: Shambhala, 1996.

Pantanjali. *Yoga: Discipline of Freedom.* Translated by Barbara Stoler Miller. California: University of California Press, 1996.

Plato. *The Republic.* Translated by Desmond Lee. London & New York: Penguin Books, Ltd., 1987.

Ramana Maharshi. *The Spiritual Teachings of Ramana Maharshi.* Boston & London: Shambhala, 1988.

Rimpoche, Sogyal. *The Tibetan Book of Living and Dying.* New York: Harper Collins, 1992.

Rimpoche, Kaul. *Luminous Mind: The Way of the Buddha.* Boston: Wisdom Publications, 1997.

Ring, Kenneth. *Life at Death: A Scientific Investigation of the Near-Death Experience.* New York: Coward, McCann, and Geoghegan, 1980.

Ring, Kenneth. *Heading Toward Omega: In Search of the Meaning of the Near-Death Experience.* New York: Morrow, 1984.

Rumi. *Feeling the Shoulder of the Lion.* Translated by Coleman Barks. Putney, Vermont: Threshold Books, 1991.

Sabom, Michael. *Recollections of Death: A Medical Investigation.* New York: Harper & Row, 1982.

Seith, V. K. *Kabir: The Weaver of God's Name.* Punjab, India: Radha Soami Satsang Beas, 1984.

Sutherland, Cherie. *Within the Light.* New York: Bantom Books, 1995.

Taylor, Jeremy. *Where People Fly and Water Runs Uphill.* New York: Warner Books, 1992.2

Mother Teresa. *In the Heart of the World.* Novato, California: New World Library, 1997.

Thurman, Robert A. F. *The Tibetan Book of the Dead.* New York: Bantam Books, 1994.

Valarino, Evelyn. *On the Other Side of Life: Exploring the Phenomenon of the Near-Death Experience.* New York & London, 1997.

Van De Castle, Robert. *Our Dreaming Mind.* New York: Random House, Inc., 1994.

Von Franz, Marie Louise. *Dreams: A Study of the Dreams of Jung, Descartes, Socrates, and Other Historical Figures.* Boston & London: Shambhala Publications, 1991.

Walsh, Roger. *The Spirit of Shamanism.* Los Angeles: Jeremy Tarcher, Inc., 1990.

Yogananda, Paramahansa. *Autobiography of a Yogi.* Los Angeles: Self-Realization Fellowship, 1946.

Yogananda, Paramahansa. *The Bhagavad Gita: Royal Science of Self-Realization.* Self-Realization Fellowship, 1995.

Zaleski, Carol. *Otherworld Journeys: Accounts of the Near-Death Experience in Medieval and Modern Times.* Oxford and New York: Oxford Press, 1987.

Robert Boldman was educated in philosophy and art at the Wright State University and has a degree in Respiratory Therapy. He has worked in pediatric critical care and related medical fields for thirty years, and lives in Ohio with his wife, Loree.

He is an internationally known author of senryu and haiku poetry (published in a dozen languages throughout the Americas, Europe, and Asia), twice winning the award "Best Book by a Single Author" from the North American Haiku Society. He is a featured poet in the THE HAIKU ANTHOLOGY (Simon & Schuster), BENEATH A SINGLE MOON: Buddhism in Contemporary American Poetry (Shambala Press), ENTER THE HEART OF THE FIRE: A Collection of Mystical Poems (California State University), and is also the author of THE ALCHEMY OF LOVE (Heartsfire Books).

His spiritual mastery embraces decades of Buddhist and Christian practice. He began experiencing the sublime energies of kundalini as a five-year-old child. At nineteen, he experienced the apex of this practice, Nirvikalpa Samadhi, and began teaching and initiating in tantra. Eventually he practiced Buddhism, meditating on emptiness and mindfulness. He then encountered a retired priest who encouraged him "just to love," binding all that he had found with love, bringing a full circle to his "search."

Mr. Boldman's unique path, spanning the East and West, emptiness and fullness, engaging life, and experiencing and working amidst near-death, undeniably qualifies him to author SACRED LIFE / HOLY DEATH: Lessons from the Near-Death Experience, a scholarly and compassionate journey through the stages of near-death that will illuminate the art of living.

HEARTSFIRE BOOKS

Life is an ongoing journey of change and evolution in all realms of existence. Our mission at Heartsfire is to help you understand life's process and to provide books that offer guidance in the search for truth, self, and clarity. We are privileged to present original and compelling writers who speak from their hearts and guide us to the magic of everyday experience. If you have a manuscript that you feel is suitable for us, we would love to hear from you. Send a letter of inquiry to: *Acquisitions Editor*, **Heartsfire Books**, 500 N. Guadalupe Street, Suite G-465, Santa Fe, New Mexico 87501 USA. Email: heartsfirebooks@heartsfirebooks.com. Visit us at http://www.heartsfirebooks.com.

Heartsfire Consciousness Literature

Creating an Abuse-Free Relationship:
A Manual for Recovering Self
and Intimacy
Carolyn McGinnis
March 1999

The Alchemy of Love:
A Pilgrimage of Sacred Discovery
Robert Boldman

The Emerald Covenant:
Spiritual Rites of Passage
Michael E. Morgan

Fathers:
Transforming Your Relationship
John Selby

Gifts from Spirit:
A Skeptic's Path
Dennis Augustine

Healing Depression:
A Guide to Making Intelligent Choices
about Treating Depression
Catherine Carrigan

Health for Life:
Secrets of Tibetan Ayurveda
Robert Sachs
Foreword by Dr. Lobsang Rapgay

Hermanos de la Luz:
Brothers of the Light
Ray John de Aragón

Inescapable Journey:
A Spiritual Adventure
Claude Saks

Sacred Life, Holy Death:
Seven Stages of Crossing the Divide
Robert Boldman
Preface by
Khenpo Konchog Gyaltshen Rinpoche
April 1999

In the Presence of My Enemies:
Memoirs of Tibetan Nobleman
Tsipon Shuguba
Sumner Carnahan with Lama Kunga
Rinpoche

Message from the Sparrows:
Engaging Consciousness
Taylor Morris

The Search for David:
A Cosmic Journey of Love
George Schwimmer

Solitude:
The Art of Living with Yourself
John Selby

Spirtuality for the Business Person:
Inner Practices for Success
Claude Saks

Strong Brew:
One Man's Prelude to Change
Claude Saks

Tibet:
Enduring Spirit, Exploited Land
Robert Z. Apte and Andrés R. Edwards
Foreword and Poem by His Holiness the
Dalai Lama